Donald Trump and Adolf Hitler: Making A Serious Comparison

By Horace Bloom

DEDICATION

This book is written in acknowledgement of the suffering
of the survivors of the Holocaust in Nazi Germany, and to
marginalized people in all societies. It is dedicated to the
preservation of the democratic ideals of liberty and
equality under the law for all people.

CONTENTS

RESPECT

This book is indebted to the historians who have chronicled the dark days of Nazi Germany and to the journalists of today who continue to detail the plans of those who would undermine our democratic institutions and abuse the power of the government.

INTRODUCTION

How dare you compare Donald Trump to Adolf Hitler!

The reaction of many people to comparisons of Donald Trump and Adolf Hitler is a simple rejection of the right to make such a comparison. To even contemplate the idea that any contemporary political leader could have some similarities to Adolf Hitler has become a cultural taboo.

When the editorial board of the Fresno State Collegian wrote that, "Trump represents the rise of a new Hitler and is capable of the same atrocities. It's like we're in the 1930s on a runaway train barreling toward World War III," readers expressed outrage, not at Trump's policies, but at the declaration that Trump and Hitler could be compared.

"I can't believe they published that! Disgraceful at best," one reader complained. "The old internet rule is that the first person in an argument to compare their opponent to Hitler automatically loses," advised another.

The taboo is a source of great temptation, however. History teacher Tom Richey paid deference to the taboo, telling his students that, "I don't want to dignify that stuff," and declaring it absurd to even to think of comparing the American Confederacy with Nazi Germany. Richey couldn't help himself, though. He went ahead and posted a satirical video to YouTube, making superficial comparisons between Adolf Hitler and Donald Trump, pointing out, for instance, that while Hitler had a goofy mustache, Trump has goofy hair on top of his head.

These kinds of glancing assessments make it easy to dismiss comparisons between Donald Trump and Adolf Hitler as absurd and unhinged. Sometimes, they certainly are. Is it, however, inherently ridiculous to make such comparisons?

There are, to put it broadly, two common reactions to the atrocities that were committed by Adolf Hitler and Nazi Germany. The first is that they must never be forgotten, that we need to keep the lessons of the Third Reich fresh in people's minds, in order to make sure that nothing like them can ever happen again.

The second reaction is to conclude that references to Adolf Hitler and the Nazi Party should be severely restricted to literal retellings of history and simple, direct condemnations. People who adhere to this line of thinking seek to place the memory of Nazi Germany into a kind of time capsule, separated from the rest of human history. In particular, they insist, current events must never be considered in the light of Nazi history, and no one should ever compare any living person to Hitler.

Justifications for the strict conceptual isolation of Nazi Germany from people who are comparable Nazis in all subsequent history include the assertion that to compare any current event to the activities of the Nazis minimizes the particular historical reality experienced by those who suffered under Hitler's rule.

For example, when James Crotty, the author of the book How To Talk American, asserts that "comparing Trump to Hitler is the worst kind of hate speech," writing that, "I find it deeply insulting to all those who died in the Holocaust to have their sacrifice cheaply denigrated in this way. When we apply a Nazi comparison to someone or something that does not fit that comparison, then Nazism and the Holocaust lose their power to shock us. And they must never lose that power. If they do, which is quickly happening right now, when something diabolical does come along again in this world, we have no way to identify it, let alone stop it, because we've cried Nazi wolf so often that the comparison has lost its power to persuade."

There is a rather circular nature to Crotty's argument. He asserts that comparing present day politicians to Hitler is "hate speech" because it makes the idea of Adolf Hitler seem too familiar, so that, when politicians come along who are like Adolf Hitler, we won't be able to meaningfully make the comparison. What Crotty fails to account for is the possibility that Donald Trump might actually have some similarities to Adolf Hitler that are worth noting.

Crotty, like other advocates of the avoidance strategy, cites something called "Godwin's Law". Unlike an actual law, the identity of Godwin's Law has a rather fluid nature, often being redefined to suit the purposes of those who use it. It began, however, as a specific idea, composed in 1990, in the form of an immutable law of physics, by Mike Godwin, a lawyer who had grown exasperated with fast any easy comparisons of practically any disliked political idea or leader to Hitler and his Nazi ideology. "As an online discussion grows longer, the probability of a comparison involving Nazis or Hitler approaches 1," Godwin wrote.

Other incarnations of Godwin's Law state things such as "If you mention Adolf Hitler or Nazis within a discussion thread, you've automatically ended whatever discussion you were taking part in," or, more simply, "Invoke the Nazis and you've lost the argument."

People who disapprove of comparisons of present-day politicians to Adolf Hitler tend to refer to Godwin's Law as if it were an actual law, or at least a cultural principle that is generally understood and accepted. However, there's never been any general cultural consensus around Godwin's Law, much less any formal establishment of the idea as an enforceable code. The premise that people who bring up comparisons of current political ideologies to the Nazis automatically lose an argument has never been agreed upon or substantiated with any empirical research.

Responding to these efforts at censorship, journalist Glenn Greenwald writes, "The very notion that a major 20th Century event like German aggression is off-limits in political discussions is both arbitrary and anti-intellectual in the extreme. There simply are instances where such comparisons uniquely illuminate important truths." Greenwald argues that the principles derived from the Nuremberg Trials were intended to be applied in the future, not "shrouded with a code of silence."

Recently, Mike Godwin himself has spoken out against the way that Godwin's Law is being used to try to stop comparisons of Donald Trump to Adolf Hitler. "If you're thoughtful about it and show some real awareness of history, go ahead and refer to Hitler or Nazis when you talk about Trump. Or any other politician," he wrote.

Godwin advised his fans that "The best way to prevent future holocausts, I believe, is not to forbear from Holocaust comparisons; instead, it's to make sure that those comparisons are meaningful and substantive."

Despite Godwin's own protestations, Godwin's Law has begun to be used as a form of censorship by followers of Trump, a tool for shutting down well-informed critiques of the candidate's policies and techniques. They're using Godwin's Law as an article of faith, and canonizing Holocaust survivors as martyrs in their efforts to stifle consideration of the broad political movement that Trump has harnessed.

The truth is that Holocaust survivors are not merely characters from the past. They're getting older, but many of them are still around.

It would be a mistake to suggest that all Holocaust survivors share the same opinions about current events in general, or Donald Trump in particular. However, it is worth noting that many survivors have spoken out about the similarities they perceive between Donald Trump and Adolf Hitler.

Eva Schloss, a former prisoner at the Auschwitz Nazi concentration camp and a sister-in-law to Anne Frank, has stated, "If Donald Trump becomes the next president of the U.S. it would be a complete disaster. I think he is acting like another Hitler by inciting racism. During his U.S. presidential campaign he has suggested the "total and complete shutdown of Muslims entering the United States," as well as pledging to build a wall between the U.S. and Mexico to keep illegal immigrants out."

Another Auschwitz survivor, Irene Weiss, explains that her concern is not about whether comparisons between Trump and Hitler are appropriate. Her concern is about the demagoguery exhibited by Donald Trump and his competitors in the 2016 presidential race. "I am exceptionally concerned about demagogues," she says. "They touch me in a place that I remember. I know their influence and, unfortunately, I know how receptive audiences are to demagogues and what it leads to."

Al Munzer, who was hidden from the Nazis as a baby, worries about Donald Trump's "message of hate," and offers a direct rebuttal to those who seek to shut down discussions of how Hitler's ideology may be manifesting itself in the campaigns of today's political leaders: "Thinking that Germany was somehow unique is wrong."

The people who fought Adolf Hitler and his armies in World War II are not honored by efforts to suppress discussions of equivalents of Hitler's actions and Nazi ideology in our own time. Greenwald points out that those who prosecuted Nazis for their war crimes after World War II did so in the hopes that people in the future would remember the Nazi atrocities, and use them as a point of comparison to maintain standards of human rights. "A primary point of the Nuremberg Trials was to seize on the extraordinary horror of what the Germans did in order to set forth general principles to be applied not only to the individual war criminals before the tribunal, but more important, to all countries in the future," he writes.

Historian Laurence Rees warned his readers that, "The desire to be led by a strong personality in a crisis, the craving for our existence to have some kind of purpose, the quasi worship of 'heroes' and 'celebrities,' the longing for salvation and redemption: none of this has changed in the world since the death of Hitler in April 1945."

The precise historical factors that allowed Adolf Hitler to establish Nazi Party to control over Germany will never be repeated. The more general cultural and social factors that led to the founding of the Third Reich, however, may well reoccur many times in the future, leading to terrifying regimes that resemble the Nazi regime in its most dreadful respects, although differing in many of the particularities of their manifestations.

There is a difference between comparing someone with Hitler and equating them with Hitler. Saying that someone is "just like Hitler" is both rhetorically extreme and factually wrong. Hitler was a unique figure in a distinct historical context. No one will ever be just like him. But someone can be enough like him that comparisons reveal significant things, and the similarities between Hitler and Donald Trump are significant enough to cause genuine concern.

Practically speaking, the horse is out of the barn. People from all kinds of backgrounds, from all around the world, are already talking about the similarities and differences between Adolf Hitler and Donald Trump. There's no centralized effort to try to manufacture these discussions. Rather, the topic is spontaneously emerging in conversations because there's something about Trump that reminds people of Hitler.

Trump himself has been confronted on the issue. George Stephanopoulos of ABC News said to Trump, "You're increasingly being compared to Hitler. Does that give you any pause at all?"

When Trump responded, he at first seemed to distance himself from the Nazi leader's ideology, but then embraced another racist atrocity of World War II – the imprisonment of American citizens of Japanese ancestry by President Franklin Roosevelt. "No," Trump responded. The comparison between himself and Hitler didn't give him pause, "because what I'm doing is not different than what FDR, FDR's solution for Germans, Italians, Japanese, many years ago... Take a look at presidential proclamations 2525, 2526, and 2527 having to do with alien Germans, alien Italians, alien Japanese, and what they did. You know, they stripped them of their naturalization proceedings. They went through a whole list of things. They couldn't go five miles from their homes. They wouldn't let them use radios, flashlights, I mean, take a look at what FDR did many years ago... I don't like doing it at all. It's a temporary measure, until representatives, many of whom are grossly incompetent, until our representatives can figure out what's going on."

In this moment, we encounter the complexity that arises when people attempt to compare a present-day political leader with Adolf Hitler. Even in denying his similarity to Hitler, Trump proposed using a discredited, racist tactic of forcing large numbers of Americans into concentration camps, as was done to Japanese-Americans during World War II.

The Americans were the enemies of Nazi Germany, of course, but the internment was like an echo of Nazi ideology here in the United States. President Roosevelt was acting something like Adolf Hitler when he signed the order to round up Japanese-Americans and treat them like criminals. So, in a literal way, Trump's response to Stephanopoulos is a rejection of his similarity to Hitler, while on a deeper level, Trump's response confirmed many Americans' concern that Trump would impose a racist, nationalist, authoritarian ideology similar to that of the Nazis if he were elected President.

This interaction shows why a serious consideration of the comparison of Donald Trump and Adolf Hitler is necessary. We won't come to an adequate understanding of this apparent historical echo through quick television interviews, short online articles, YouTube videos, and pugnacious candidate debates. Through such resources, we are exposed to a small piece of a much larger, more complex cultural dynamic.

American voters, and the concerned citizens of the world, are struggling to form a broader and deeper understanding of Donald Trump, to understand how to react to him. We have never seen an American presidential candidate like him before. It is the goal of this book to help provide, through the context of the darkest chapter of the last hundred years, a different kind of insight into the kind of leader that Trump might become, if we allow him to rise to power.

CHAPTER 2:
THE BIOGRAPHIES OF
TRUMP AND HITLER

"Many people have stated that Adolf Hitler was evil, mad, or crazy. The really scary thing is that Hitler was a man." – Jennifer Rosenberg

Photograph by Heinrich Hoffmann, in the public domain

The strange thing about Adolf Hitler is that he was at the simultaneously terrifyingly powerful and ridiculous. For an epitome of pure evil, he was extremely easy to snicker at, from a distance.

One of the most common rebuttals to Trump-Hitler comparisons is to state that, while Adolf Hitler killed millions of people, Donald Trump only says mean things about people. Obviously, according to this line of reasoning, there can be no comparison between the two.

Such dismissals miss an essential point, however: Adolf Hitler did not kill millions of people before he became Chancellor of Germany. He did so after he gained control over the government.

The comparison of Adolf Hitler at the height of Nazi power in Germany with Donald Trump before he is elected President of the United States is indeed absurd. The apt comparison is between Donald Trump as he campaigns for President of the United States and Adolf Hitler before he gained any political office. When this comparison is made, important distinctions between the two politicians remain, but the idea of assessing the similarities between them no longer seems quite so ridiculous.

The essential question that this book confronts is not whether Donald Trump is like a brutal dictator who has imposed a harsh totalitarian regime over his own nation and unleashed a terrible war against other nations. The essential question for voters in 2016 is whether Donald Trump could become a dictator of this sort. The matter under consideration is whether, in electing Donald Trump as President of the United States, the American people would be making a similar mistake as was made by the Germans who allowed Adolf Hitler to become Chancellor of their nation.

It may seem silly to suppose that Donald Trump could ever make himself anything like a dictator over the USA. However, the apparently ludicrous nature of this scenario is actually one of the most fundamental similarities between the political ascent of Adolf Hitler and the political ascent of Donald Trump.

In his account of the rise and fall of Adolf Hitler, Laurence Rees observed, "In 1913, when Adolf Hitler was twenty-four years old, nothing about his life marked him out as a future charismatic leader." To most people outside Germany, Hitler seemed like nothing more than a cruel clown until he attained the position of Chancellor.

Photograph by Heinrich Hoffmann, in the public domain

Adolf Hitler was easy to dismiss precisely because he was outlandish in both his mannerisms and his ideas. The same cartoonish demeanor led many Americans to presume in June 2015 that Donald Trump's presidential candidacy was nothing more than a joke, or a casual bit of self-indulgence that would quickly flame out. Only in hindsight can we see that the Trump for President campaign was never anything of the sort.

Let us now put aside the facile dismissals of the

Trump-Hitler comparison, and make a serious consideration of the matter. This chapter begins by examining the biographies of the two leaders.

A biographical comparison of Adolf Hitler and Donald Trump needs to begin with an some debunking of some false claims about supposedly direct links between Donald Trump and Adolf Hitler. In December 2015, a satirical web site published an article declaring that Donald Trump is closely related to Adolf Hitler – that Trump's paternal grandmother was married to Hitler's grand uncle, Johann Schicklgruber.

This story is completely fictional. It was made up as a joke, and unfortunately, some people have been too dense to see it for that.

Even if the story were true, it would be irrelevant. It might be important if Adolf Hitler were revealed to be Donald Trump's secret grandfather, but the idea that there could be some taint for Trump that comes from being a distant cousin of Hitler is ridiculous. Raving nationalism is not known to be a genetic trait that can be passed down from generation to generation through simple biological ancestry.

It is true that Donald Trump has a significant amount of German heritage, but that's true of the majority of Americans. People with German ancestry are the largest ethnic group in the United States.

In the interest of disclosure, I'll share the fact with you that one of my own family, an uncle on my mother's side, was a general in the Nazi military during World War II. That doesn't make me a Nazi. Here I am, despite this connection to Hitler's army, writing a book with the fundamental principle that the Third Reich was a terrible stain on world history.

As a person of German ancestry, Donald Trump does share one interesting piece of history – the transformation of his family name. In the case of the Nazi Fuhrer, the change was from Hiedler to Hitler. In the case of the billionaire Republican presidential candidate, the change was to Trump from Drumpf.

One wonders if Donald Trump might have grown up with a smaller tendency toward self-aggrandizement if his last name had sounded more like a tired sigh instead of representing a special ability to transcend ordinary limits in a game of cards. We will, of course, never know if this would have been the case.

A second false claim linking Donald Trump to the Nazi Party has been built upon a conspiracy theory spread by a large number of right wing media organizations, including Fox News and Investor's Business Daily. You see a representation of it in this graphic, which has been widely distributed through social media:

The charge that Donald Trump and Barack Obama are quite serious. As such, these charges require substantial proof. If people are going to accuse Donald Trump of secretly being controlled by George Soros, who is then alleged to be a "former Nazi sympathizer", then they had better be able to come up with concrete evidence that their allegations are true.

Conspiracy theories about a New World Order, although they are sometimes posed in terms of opposition to Nazi ideology, as in the example above, actually advance a central tenet of Nazi ideology: The belief that wealthy Jews secretly control the entire world. Although the conspiracy theory claims to be shocked that George Soros would collaborate with the Nazis, it is itself a propaganda tool of those promoting an antisemitism that the Nazis would have admired.

For confirmation of this interpretation, we can go directly to the center of NeoNazi activity online – the Stormfront web site. "Lrapsody", a sustaining member of Stormfront, repeats the Trump-Soros-Nazi conspiracy, but from a different angle, writing that, "Trump owes a lot of money to Jew George Soros and other wall street Jews. He is completely disingenuous. Seems the Jews have fooled a few with their new star puppet."

In this version of the conspiracy theory alleging that Soros controls Donald Trump, Soros is given the role of representing "the Jews", and not the Nazis at all. The conspiracy theory is so dominated by its own hate that it twists itself into garbled chains of flawed logic that lead nowhere but deep into incoherence.

If Barack Obama and Donald Trump were actually controlled by a single puppet master, they would support the same policies, but on most issues, Obama and Trump are on opposite sides. Obama is pro-choice, Trump is pro-life. Obama is pro-regulation, Trump is anti-regulation. Obama is for fighting climate change, Trump refuses to acknowledge even that climate change exists. You get the picture.

Finally, all existing evidence about the political preferences of George Soros in the 2016 presidential election points to the conclusion that Soros is a determined opponent of Donald Trump, rather than his puppet master. In December 2015, Soros expressed his opposition to the election of Donald Trump in an editorial published in The Guardian, writing that "as 2016 gets underway, we must reaffirm our commitment to the principles of open society and resist the siren song of the likes of Donald Trump and Ted Cruz, however hard that may be."

Aside from this conspiracy theory's lack of structural integrity, its most alarming premise is not supported by the evidence that's available to us. The single information source used by people repeating the story contradicts the allegations of Nazi collaboration. What's more, the testimony of witnesses who observed George Soros during World War II shows that he was a fugitive from the Nazis, rather than their partner in the Holocaust.

It is alleged by proponents of the New World Order conspiracy theory that George Soros chose to go around Budapest, posing as a Christian, while helping Nazis to loot the homes of wealthy Jewish families that were forced to flee. This allegation is entirely based upon an interview of George Soros conducted on the CBS TV show 60 Minutes by Steve Kroft back in 1998.

In this interview, Kroft kept questioning Soros about whether he felt any sense of guilt for having gone out with a representative of the Nazis in Hungary, and, in the words of Kroft, "helped in the confiscation of property from the Jews".

Soros stammered, and responded that, "Well, of course I could be on the other side or I could be the one from whom the thing is being taken away. But there was no sense that I shouldn't be there, because that was, well, actually, in a funny way, it's just like in markets, that if I weren't there, of course, I wasn't doing it, but somebody else would, would, would be taking it away anyhow. And it was the -- whether I was there or not, I was only a spectator, the property was being taken away. So the, I had no role in taking away that property. So I had no sense of guilt."

This sounds pretty damning. It sounds as if, during

World War II, George Soros took on a job in which he worked with the Nazis to steal from Jewish families that were being shipped off to concentration camps. It's sounds downright evil.

Things begin to sound quite different when more of the truth about what George Soros did under the Nazi occupation of Hungary is revealed.

For one thing, at the time of the episode that 60 Minutes questioned Soros about, he was just a 14 year-old boy.

For another thing, Soros wasn't in the habit of going out to the homes of "the Jews" and stealing their property in the name of the Nazi regime. He went out to only one Jewish home, the extensive estate of a wealthy Jewish family, the Kornfelds, that had fled the country.

Also, Soros didn't actually help loot the home. He walked around the estate, talked to staff members, and rode horse, and then left.

Finally, there's the reason that Soros traveled to that home: Soros had been separated from his family. When the Nazis invaded Hungary, Soros had been left at the home of an Christian employee of the Hungarian Agricultural Ministry with the name of Baumbach. His father paid Baumbach to pretend that Soros was his son.

In order to survive, George Soros had to pretend that he was a Christian, and that his name was Sandor Kiss. Baumbach was given the odious task of looting homes of Jewish families, and had Soros accompany him to the Kornfeld estate, because the trip would take Baumbach three days. Baumbach was afraid that if he left Soros alone back at his house, he might be discovered, and seized, and taken off to a concentration camp.

So, the conspiracy theory that states that Donald Trump is being secretly controlled by a Nazi collaborator, who in turn is working for a Jewish New World Order cabal, is completely bogus. Soros wasn't a Nazi collaborator, but a fugitive from the Nazis. The Jewish

New World Order is itself a neoNazi fantasy.

Such ridiculous conspiracy theories should remind us that, in making comparisons between Donald Trump and Adolf Hitler, it is easy to slip into wild, irresponsible conjecture. That's not the kind of comparison that this book seeks to make. If the comparisons are to have any value, it will be essential to stick to the facts, without distortion.

To begin the serious comparison of the biographies of Donald Trump and Adolf Hitler, it is essential to acknowledge some remarkable differences between the two men. These differences begin with their status at birth.

Adolf Hitler was born poor. His father worked hard to financially-struggling, socially obscure family with a history of peasant labor.

William Shirer, a journalist who lived in Germany through the rise of the Nazi power into the Third Reich, explains that Hitler was born into a family with little money to spare, and descended into even greater poverty when he moved to Vienna as a young man. "he lived in flophouses or in the almost equally miserable quarters of the men's hostel," Shirer writes, "staving off hunger by frequenting the charity soup kitchens of the city."

Whatever we think of what he made of himself, no one can deny that Hitler was a true self-made man. He rose to absolute authority from absolute obscurity, sometimes even sleeping outside on park benches in a threadbare coat because he had nowhere else to go.

People often poke fun at Hitler's initial career as an artist, and it's true that he wasn't very successful. He was denied admittance into art school, and his paintings never sold for much money. Most of them were sold merely as place fillers to merchants who found that they could sell picture frames more readily when if there was already a painting within them.

This much must be said for Hitler: was able to keep

himself alive with his painting work. He started the business nearly from nothing. The only financial support he ever received for this venture from his family was a small bit of money from his aunt – enough to buy some paint and brushes.

Though he considered himself German, the future Fuhrer wasn't even born in Germany. He was born on the border of Bavaria and Austria, in the minor town of Braunau am Inn. His later Anschluss of Austria into Germany has widely been interpreted as a consequence of his childhood in these borderlands, looking in to Germany from the outside.

It's difficult to imagine how the birth of Donald Trump could be more different from Hitler's. Unlike his opponent, Ted Cruz, he was born squarely inside the borders of the United States, to a family living in New York City.

Donald Trump was born rich. His father, Fred Trump, made a fortune as a real estate developer, and provided an easy path into a lucrative business.

By the time that Donald Trump graduated from college, he was already a millionaire. While at the Wharton School of Business, Trump was able to make a healthy amount of money through a business project at an apartment complex that had been bought by his father for 5.7 million dollars. Adolf Hitler could have never dreamed of receiving such a huge investment in his early career.

When Trump graduated from school, he didn't have to struggle to find work. His father gave him a good paying job with excellent opportunities for advancement at his real estate business.

Despite these extreme economic advantages, Trump claims that his story is one of overcoming hardship. "My whole life really has been a 'no' and I fought through it," Trump told a crowd of his supporters recently. "It has not been easy for me. It has not been easy for me, and you know I started off in Brooklyn. My father gave me a small loan of a million dollars."

Though he enjoyed a life of luxury later in life, to young Adolf Hitler, a loan of a million dollars would have felt in no way "small". In that way, Hitler was more like most Americans, who can expect no more assistance from their parents upon graduation than a few thousand dollars.

Even if Hitler's father had been more financially successful, it is doubtful that he would have granted his son a million dollar loan. Unlike Trump, who idolized his father, Hitler detested his father, who had beaten him regularly from a young age.

Hitler was determined to get away from his father as soon as possible, not just to escape the physical blows, but evade being sucked into his father's professional status. The elder Hitler was proud of his job as a civil servant, but young Adolf saw such a career as like a prison. He dreamed of being a "master of my own time." Writing his manifesto and memoir Mein Kampf, Hitler recalled, "I did not want to become a civil servant, no, and again no. All attempts on my father's part to inspire me with love or pleasure in this profession by stories from his own life accomplished the exact opposite."

Hitler's defiance of his father's authority was mirrored by his opposition to the authority of the adults at school. His teachers soon came to regard him as "argumentative, autocratic, self-opinionated and bad-tempered, and unable to submit to school discipline."

Trump shared Hitler's tendency toward behavioral problems in school, but these difficulties led to vastly different consequences, because Trump had a wealthy father. Fred Trump was on the board of trustees of the private school that his son attended, and so held some influence over matters of discipline when the adolescent Donald got into trouble.

Eventually, when his son's behavior became too disturbing to sweep under the rug any longer, Fred Trump sent Donald to a private military boarding school, the New

York Military Academy, 60 miles up the Hudson River from Manhattan.

The Hitler family didn't have enough money to send their son to a private boarding school, so Adolf could only remain in a school where his studied would be directed to the learning of the skills necessary to establish him in a mediocre post as a civil servant. There was to be no training in the skills he would need to become the artist he aspired to be.

Hitler was stuck, and so, he engaged in the only form of protest available to him. He refused to study for his classes, hoping that his father would break down and allow him to finally train as a painter.

There was, alas, no compromise. So, although Hitler had consistently good grades before the conflict with his father, they degraded to the state of nearly complete failure. Hitler dropped out before he could graduate, and drifting for a few years after his father's early death before finally leaving for Vienna.

In contrast, once he arrived at the elite military academy, Trump seemed to accept the will of his father, whom he became determined to emulate. Trump graduated at the top of his class. Whatever his advantages, here is no denying that Trump possesses a sharp mind.

Whereas Hitler drifted through a series of short-lived jobs before building up his small living as a painter, Trump remained in school, attending Fordham University before transferring to the Wharton School of Business to gain a degree in real estate. Unlike Hitler, Trump was perfectly happy to pursue a degree designed to gain him admittance to his father's line of work.

Although Trump was an able student in his younger days, as an adult he has drifted into the same anti-intellectual pose adopted by Hitler. Urging his voters to turn out and participate in a Republican caucus, Trump distanced himself from the political sophistication of GOP insiders, telling his audience that, "I'm not going to use the word 'caucus' I'm just going to use just 'vote'. What the hell is caucus? Nobody even knows what that means."

Of course, plenty of people understand what caucuses are, and how they work. That isn't the point. Trump derives pleasure, as Hitler did, in mocking the learning of others.

Not long after their schooling was done, both Hitler and Trump faced a gut-wrenching decision: Whether to fight for their countries in war. When World War I came, Adolf Hitler requested to be allowed to fight in the German army, even though was not a German citizen. Under no obligation to do so, he risked his life to save his brothers in arms, was injured on the battlefield, and earned a medal for his courage.

When his educational deferments ran out, Donald Trump sought a medical excuse not to go and fight in Vietnam. Trump had received military training at his elite private academy, but he was reluctant to put it into practice. Even though an initial medical examination found him physically fit for military duty, giving him A-1 status, a second medical examination conducted shortly before he was to be eligible for the draft lottery discovered a minor medical defect in his feet, enabling Trump to evade going to Vietnam. "Bone spurs," the doctor called it.

There's nothing wrong with people deciding not to join in a war that they disagree with, or to abstain from violence completely due to deeply held philosophical principles. That's not what appears to have motivated Donald Trump, however. Trump seems to simply have wanted to avoid putting his own skin at risk.

Not all future politicians made Trump's choice, of course. Secretary of State John Kerry volunteered to fight in Vietnam. So did Senator John McCain – not that this decision impresses Trump.

"He's not a war hero," Trump said of Senator McCain in 2015, shortly after declaring the beginning of his presidential campaign. "I like people who weren't captured."

It is true that John McCain had been a prisoner of war in Vietnam before beginning his political career, but capture had nothing to do with a lack of heroism. His plane was struck by a missile over Hanoi. He broke both arms and one leg ejecting from the plane, and landed in a lake. After being pulled ashore he was captured by the North Vietnamese, who stabbed him with a bayonet and crushed his shoulder with a rifle butt. He was held prisoner for over five years, during which time he received minimal medical care and was repeatedly tortured. It is simply not plausible to claim that someone who was more of a "hero" could have somehow avoided capture.

Trump's dismissal of John McCain's suffering in a prisoner of war camp seemed particularly cruel given Trump's enthusiasm for reinstating George W. Bush's programs of torture against prisoners of war, which have been ended under President Barack Obama. After hearing this blunt insult against a well-respected Republican U.S. Senator and former presidential candidate, most political pundits assumed that Trump's presidential campaign had ended, almost before it had begun. The Republican Party, after all, prided itself upon showing conspicuous respect to military veterans, in word if not always in deed.

Strangely, the pundits were soon proven wrong. Donald Trump's ratings in public opinion polls of likely Republican voters didn't decrease at all after the jab at McCain. In fact, Trump's ratings in a few of the polls began to rise.

These days, Trump seems to have changed his feelings about violence. Now that he is too old to fight himself, he has become all-too-eager to send young men off to kill and be killed in war. His foreign policy is summed up with his phrase, "I would bomb the shit out of them!" This enthusiasm for military action is one of the few points where the biographies of Donald Trump and Adolf Hitler

22

begin to converge.

Certainly, the paths to power chosen by the two leaders were not the same. Trump has ascended to prominence through business, referring to himself as "the archetypal businessman". Hitler, lacking the hereditary capital needed to make a quick launch into the business world, decided upon politics as his route to greatness.

Despite the different professional spheres through which Hitler and Trump advanced, they shared in common the development of a particular oratory style. Both leaders have succeeded in building large followings through a bombastic, flamboyant approach to their speeches, exciting their audiences into explosive displays of emotion that sometimes erupt into violence. While Hitler's speeches are more formal than Trump's, both speakers use wild gestures and exaggerated facial expressions to keep their audiences enthralled. The speeches of both men use superlative language to convey a sense of urgent need, while avoiding wonky policy details.

Above all else, Trump and Hitler both rely upon the power of emphatic assertion, not worrying about providing evidence for their claims of truth. They use overpowering confidence to cultivate a sense of trust within people listening to them. "Believe me," Trump tells his audiences, over and over again. They do.

Trump seems to believe in himself as much as his rank and file supporters do. He once declared to Jimmy Fallon, on The Tonight Show, that, "I think apologizing's a great thing, but you have to be wrong. I will absolutely apologize, sometime in the hopefully distant future, if I'm ever wrong."

It is possible that the similarities between the energetic speaking styles of Hitler and Trump are due to something more than mere happenstance. In 1990, Donald Trump's first wife, Ivana, divulged that her husband kept a collection of Hitler's speeches, titled My New Order, in a cabinet by his side of the bed. Marty Davis, an entertainment executive, confirmed that he had given Trump a copy of the book.

When confronted about his creation of a special place for Hitler's speeches in his bedroom, Donald Trump explained that it wasn't a big deal, because Davis was a Jew. In fact, says Davis, "I am his friend, but I'm not Jewish."

Photo by Gage Skidmore

CHAPTER 3:
THE HISTORY OF WEIMAR GERMANY AND THE USA TODAY

Whether Donald Trump, as an individual, is similar to Adolf Hitler is not the ultimate concern for American voters. It is the social movement that Trump represents that matters most.

All of the cruel destruction that Hitler inflicted would have been impossible without other people, in almost every segment of German society, willing to do his bidding. In another time, in another place, in another culture, Adolf Hitler would have been unknown to history, confined to a marginal role, his irrational fury unable to harm anyone but the few of the people immediately around him.

To understand whether the threat to peace and freedom posed by Donald Trump is anything similar to the threat that was posed by Adolf Hitler, it is necessary to consider how much the United States today has in common with the Weimar Republic of Germany, from which Hitler and the Nazi Party rose to power. What we need most is to understand whether the USA is likely to allow Trump to run away with power as Hitler did in Germany.

This comparison brings cause for hope, because there are some profound differences between the United States today and Germany in the 1920s and 1930s.

The most fundamental difference has to do with national stability. For generations, the United States has been a well-established nation, with a solid and stable identity. Not since the Civil War, a century and a half ago, has this identity faced a serious challenge, either from within or without.

Germany, on the other hand, was barely more than an abstract concept when Hitler rose to power. During the Weimar Republic, the national government was weak, with the leaders of Germany's constituent states constantly testing central authority. Germany had been a region of separate sovereign states for centuries, and then a loose confederation before its brief status as an empire.

During Hitler's young life, many Germans didn't live within the borders of Germany at all, and many of those who lived within Germany didn't really think of themselves as such. There were Prussians and Bavarians... and there were Jews. Hitler's assertion that he was, though born in Austria, a true German, was always in dispute, through the dispute went underground after the Anschluss.

Germany was still in a process of becoming itself when Hitler made his way onto the political stage. As a result, many of the basic tenets of how Germany could be governed were still up for debate.

In the United States, we have lived under the same Constitution for well over two hundred years. That Constitution has been amended, and our understanding of how the Constitution should be applied as shifted, but the core legal principles of American government have remained the same since shortly after the Revolution of

1776. The longevity of our Bill of Rights and other liberties places a more substantial barrier in the way of a would-be American despot than what Hitler had to surmount.

The democratic idealism that held the Weimar Republic together consisted of mere wisps compared to the marble columns of democracy in the United States. In the years when Hitler scrambled to national prominence, it was not at all uncommon for German politicians to openly sneer at the weakness of democracy. It may be an exaggeration to say that aspiring dictators were a dime a dozen, but not much of one. Many Germans were even seeking the restoration of monarchy.

Unlike the Germans of the early 20th century, we Americans do not live in a culture where the display of a strong man's power places him above and beyond the normal system of rules. In our country, no one is above the law. In the Weimar Republic, the law bent in different ways for different people.

If an American organized an armed rebellion against the U.S. federal government, that person would be punished harshly, perhaps even executed for treason. Even the Bundy brothers, who couldn't manage to do more than establish an armed occupation of a government bird sanctuary gift shop which was closed for the winter, are being tried on felony conspiracy charges.

There is one sphere of American society, however, in which disdain for liberty, equality and the rule of law equals that seen in Weimar Germany: The realm of popular entertainment. Donald Trump has been practicing political tactics in this arena for years, as the star of a pair of unreal reality shows on TV – Apprentice and Celebrity Apprentice.

Fact and fantasy are blended in theatrically compelling ways on these shows, in which Trump portrays a fictional version of himself: A chief executive with absolute power.

Magician Penn Jillette, who appeared as a contestant on one of these shows, explained that, "No one can tell you the rules of Celebrity Apprentice. No one. Donald Trump just does what he wants, which is mostly pontificating to people who are sucking up to him."

On his TV shows, Trump has no anxious investors, no board of directors to answer to, nobody to check his authority in any way. No one on these shows has any power at all to contest his catch phrase declaration of authority: "You're fired!"

The actual business ventures featured on The Apprentice are very small in scale. Contestants are put in charge of minor tasks like organizing a small reception, running a retail store for a few days, or selling candy on the street. These businesses are only significant as proving grounds for people who aspire to the servitude of apprenticeship to Trump. The contrived drama of Apprentice is designed to exhibit the subservience of all before the power of Trump, much as Nazi rallies were designed to display the absolute authority of Hitler over everyone involved.

In the actual business of The Apprentice, Trump is far from all-powerful. He has to answer to network executives and advertisers. In the real world of The Apprentice, Trump has been fired.

Ironically, it was Trump's disparaging comments about immigrants caused him to lose his job and be replaced by an immigrant. Arnold Schwarzenegger is scheduled to host Celebrity Apprentice in the 2016-2017 season.

Trump, by becoming a Republican presidential candidate, has merely moved onto a larger stage. Trump has smoothly transitioned this persona from reality TV to his presidential candidacy. While other candidates look visibly uncomfortable trading their power suits for nylon jackets when talking to working class crowds, Trump casually mismatches class symbols by wearing a baseball hats with expensive suits. He is a billionaire populist, who appeals to the masses not in spite of, but because of, his elite status. He does not promise a return of power to average citizens, or a revitalization of democracy. Instead, he promises to wield absolute power on behalf of America. For people who feel powerless, and see little prospect of becoming powerful in the future, this promise is appealing.

"You know, I get greedy. I want money, money. Now, I'm going to - I'll tell you what we're going to do, right? We get greedy, right?" Trump told his followers after his victory in the Nevada caucus. "Now we're going to get greedy for the United States. We're going to grab and grab and grab." Through statements like these, Trump gives permission to his followers to express their shameful desires.

The collective joy experienced by people in the crowds at Trump rallies comes from the release of dark emotions that Americans are ordinarily encouraged to suppress. Barely controlled anger, is a feature shared by the popular movements behind both Hitler and Trump. Donald Trump's campaign rallies have become infamous for their eruptions of mob violence against anti-Trump protesters. At times, Trump seems to encourage the attacks. After one rally, at which Trump supporters repeatedly attacked an African-American man while Trump himself shouted, "get him out of here," the candidate was unapologetic. "Maybe he should have been roughed up, because it was absolutely disgusting what he was doing," he told a reporter.

At another rally, when a protester was forced out of the arena, Trump roared to the crowd, "The guards are being very gentle with him. I'd like to punch him in the face, I'll tell you that!" Thousands of supporters shouted their approval, and then Trump told them, "You know what they used to do to a guy like that in a place like this? They'd be carried out on a stretcher, folks."

The violent rage within crowds of Trump supporters had its equivalent in Hitler's Nazi gatherings. Hitler himself bragged about it, writing in Mein Kampf, about a particular outburst, "There was a hail of shouts, there were violent clashes in the hall, a handful of the most faithful war comrades and other supporters battled with the disturbers… Communists and Socialists… and only little by little were able to restore order. I was able to go on speaking."

Of course, the Nazis weren't just violent in the arenas. They were bloody out on the streets as well. Nazi militias engaged in armed clashes with gangs from other political parties. We've seen only little hints of this kind of brutality from the supporters of Donald Trump – such as when he inspired one of his fans to beat a homeless Hispanic man with a metal pole. The attacker told police afterwards that "Donald Trump was right, all these illegals need to be deported," although the victim was a U.S. citizen.

This attack was deplorable, but Nazi violence took on quite a different scale. Kristallnacht didn't take place until 5 years after Adolf Hitler seized power, but there were Nazi brutalities all over Germany while the Nazis were on the rise. So far, we aren't seeing that much widespread violence from mobs of Trump supporters.

Furthermore, the United States doesn't have a might-makes-right political culture in which political parties established squads of armed, uniformed goons. It wasn't just the Nazi Party that had these in Weimar Germany.

Political violence wasn't restricted to the attacks and intimidation by individuals or gangs, either. The German political atmosphere in the 1920s and 1930s was extremely volatile. Attempted coups d'etat were not uncommon.

A devastated economy was one factor that fueled this violence. There are serious, systemic problems in the American economy in our time. However, the state of the economy in the Weimar Republic was far worse than the state of the American economy is now.

Toward the end of the republic, inflation had made the German currency practically worthless. Unemployment was pervasive – and even those Germans who had work couldn't pay for the necessities of life. Bread lines stretched out into the streets. The economic crisis was so grave that German society was on the verge of falling apart. On top of the global Great Depression, Germany was compelled to pay crippling reparations to the countries it had attacked in World War I.

Germany's military defeat was the other factor that contributed to the roiling brutality of political life in the Weimar Republic. Donald Trump is fond of saying that America doesn't win anything any more (in fact, he's been saying this since the 1980s), but the losses Trump cites are microscopic in comparison to what Germany dealt with in 1918.

World War I had been savage for every nation involved, with extremely high numbers of fatalities and terribly wounded men. The fighting was more intense than anything anyone had ever seen before, amplified by terrible new weapons. For Germany, to have lost the war after all this suffering was profoundly traumatic. Huge numbers of soldiers returned to Germans towns and cities in a state of profound psychological disturbance. The entire society was a wreck. The United States has suffered nothing of the sort.

In historical fact, there are strong differences between Weimar Germany and the United States today. However, there are strong similarities in the way that many Americans today perceive the status of their nation and of their individual place in the world.

"We're a third world nation," Trump writes. Of course, this is a silly, ignorant thing to say. The United States is an economic superpower, and Americans on the whole live in great luxury compared to the conditions endured by much of the rest of the world. Only an out-of-touch billionaire could believe that the conditions in America are anything like those of a genuine third world nation.

What is true is that Americans feel economically deprived. They feel alienated in their workplaces, where corporate efficiency schemes increasingly squeeze the humanity out of their labor. They feel simultaneously dazzled and disoriented by the rapid changes wrought by racing developments in digital technology.

Republicans in particular feel unsettled by cultural changes such as the embrace of equal rights for homosexuals and the slow decline of American Christianity. What for many other Americans feels like a liberation seems to them a terrifying dissolution of the bedrock upon which civilization is founded.

Furthermore, for American racists, who are not insubstantial in number, the presidency of Barack Obama has provoked a psychological crisis. They have been confronted, year after year, with a competent, respected man with dark skin who has been able to repeatedly outmaneuver his light-skinned opponents. In the minds of racists, such a thing ought not to be possible.

Some racists have responded by softening their hatred. Most, however, have merely twisted their anger into new, more uncomfortable forms. To compensate for the unavoidable political supremacy of a successful African-American, they have developed large numbers of outlandish conspiracy theories that, if they were not so collective, would be regarded as a manifestation of insanity.

Republican social networks are flooded with extreme stories of abuse of power and looming calamity. These stories claim that Barack Obama has purposefully allowed Muslim terrorists into the United States, carrying carrying nuclear suitcase bombs that are about to be detonated. It doesn't matter that these stories have been repeated over and over throughout President Obama's two terms in office, and have never come true or been substantiated in any form. To many Republican voters, they feel true.

The stories tell of Obama's plan to introduce the Ebola virus, a potent symbol of African identity gone out of control, to the United States. They tell of secret concentration camps that have been built across the United States by the Federal Emergency Management Agency. They tell of the secret movement of American soldiers across the United States and military training exercises that will soon impose martial law. They simultaneously tell of strict Islamic sharia law being imposed, and of ministers being forced to marry gay couples. There have even been widespread rumors spread among Republican voters of guillotines being secretly installed in communities across America, to be used in the slaughter of American Christians that is soon to come.

In a cultural context where such wild tales are given credence, Trump's vision of an America that has been defeated doesn't require consistency in either logic or facts. It merely needs to represent an emotional truth. Trump's supporters genuinely feel that their country has gone to hell in a handbasket, and requires a powerful hand to guide it back into victory, solvency and righteousness.

Trump shares in this emotionally-driven cognitive dissonance. Within a single paragraph, Trump writes that, "We have to take it back, we have to take our country back. We've lost our jobs, we've lost our money," and that "I have some of the great assets of the world." These two assertions of truth, that Donald Trump possesses "great assets" and that "we" have lost "our money", are rationally incompatible, but that doesn't matter to Trump and his supporters. What matters is that both assertions feel true, and that they point to a fundamental wrong in the world that must be put right: That America is a wealthy nation that nonetheless feels impoverished.

Among Republicans, the source of this conflict is the combination of the reality of economic struggle with two of their political party's central creeds: 1) that the United States is the greatest nation on Earth, and 2) that the United States is a meritocracy. If the United States really was both the greatest nation on Earth and a meritocracy, then there wouldn't be any economic problems for any hard-working American.

What most Americans actually experience is that their hard work often doesn't pay off in the end. Since the Great Recession, the wealthiest Americans have grown ever more wealthy, while the rest of America, including not just the poor but also the middle class, has been forced to work longer hours for less money. What's more, for decades, worker productivity has been rising, while wages have been falling. This combination of statistics shows that investors and business owners, such as Trump, have been squeezing wealth from workers in an increasingly raw deal.

Many American workers, however, don't want to blame American financial elites for their economic struggles. That's because their sense of individual power relies upon the feeling that they can improve their economic condition through sheer effort, regardless of the obstacles. Without this belief, many working Americans simply wouldn't feel able to go on.

As a result, the message of Donald Trump holds a special appeal. Instead of acknowledging that it's people like himself, within the USA, that have taken wealth from working Americans, Trump blames outsiders. He blames immigrants. He blames China. He blames Barack Obama for failing to stand up to China. He declares that American workers need is a strongman to get tough and demand a better deal, when in fact, it's the strongmen of American business who have stripped the wealth out of working Americans' lives in the first place.

It's politically appealing to blame outsiders for working Americans' economic problems, because outsiders can be dealt with more simply, with a posture of toughness. Admitting that the problem may lie within the American system itself requires people to acknowledge flaws that are closer to home, when they are already feeling vulnerable.

The fractured, irrational vision of a fundamental wrong that drives American workers to support Trump's economic scapegoating is strikingly similar to the belief harbored by many Germans of Hitler's generation that the German military had been "stabbed in the back" at the end of World War I. These Germans, many of whom, like Hitler, were in the field when their country was forced to surrender, had an ardent faith in the superiority of the German military. Lacking a broader vision of the war, they only saw that their individual units seemed to be holding their own against the enemy.

When the order came to stand down, and the news arrived that Germany was surrendering under humiliating terms, German soldiers were outraged. They refused to believe that their own military, their own fighting had been in vain, that they had risked their lives, enduring terror and sacrifice for years, for nothing. It was easier for them to find someone else, someone non-German, to blame.

So it was that Adolf Hitler, and many others in his position, found the psychological power of redirecting their frustration against Jews. It was easier for them to believe that they had been betrayed by a cabal of Jews that secretly controlled Germany than to believe that Germany had failed itself by launching a war that it could not sustain. The Jews, after all, would be easy to defeat. There were more Germans than Jews, after all.

For a while, the anti-Semitic fantasy energized the Germans who believed in it. It brought the Nazis to power and enabled a burst of military revitalization. However, in the end, the pursuit of phantom Jewish puppet masters brought Germany to disaster again.

It is too early to say whether the United States will be wrecked by an irrational pursuit of convenient scapegoats in the way that Germany was ruined by its irrational hunger for Jewish blood. What we can observe is that the presidential campaign of Donald Trump has identified several vulnerable populations as convenient scapegoats, and is readying Americans for a purge.

If this sounds ominous, consider what's at stake in this

presidential contest. Nations all over the Earth suffered terribly during World War II, but the weaponry now held in the militaries of the world makes the armaments used by the Nazis seem insignificant.

When Adolf Hitler took power, the German military was much weaker than that of its European rivals. Donald Trump, if he gains the White House, will inherit a military that is several times stronger than all the other militaries on the planet combined – and he plans to make it even more powerful.

As much as the Allies worried about the possibility, Adolf Hitler was never able to develop nuclear weapons. If Donald Trump were elected President of the United States, he would have thousands of nuclear weapons at his disposal, each one many times more powerful than the atomic bombs the American military dropped on Hiroshima and Nagasaki.

If Donald Trump were to lose his temper, made to feel that he had come out the loser in a negotiation, or decide on a whim to improvise…

…that could be the end for us all.

Photo by Gage Skidmore

CHAPTER 4:
IDEOLOGIES OF THE
NAZIS AND DONALD TRUMP

"We're going to have to do things that we never did before... and certain things will be done that we never thought would happen in this country." – Donald Trump

That there are differences between the biographical and historical contexts of Adolf Hitler's rise to power and Donald Trump's presidential campaign is reassuring. The similarities between the ideologies crafted by the Nazis and Donald Trump, however, are disturbing.

At the core of these similarities is an extreme nationalism, fueled by xenophobia. The particular outsiders loathed by Hitler and Trump are different, but the tenor of their loathing is the same.

The Nazi rise to power was fueled by an ancient ideology of antipathy toward Jews, constructed out of an elaborate system of delusions of persecution. Among these delusions was the blood libel.

The blood libel was the false belief that Jews routinely kidnap Christian children in order to kill them and drain them of blood, which is subsequently used for secret Jewish rituals. Although the blood libel predated the Third Reich by hundreds of years, its impact reached an unprecedented scale under the Nazis, who used it as an excuse for the barbarities of the Holocaust.

There is no evidence that Donald Trump has ever uttered the ancient blood libel against Jews in any form. He has been accused of indulging in negative stereotypes of Jews on occasion, but if Trump is anti-Semitic, he is not blatant about it. However, Trump has engaged in equivalents of the blood libel against other groups.

Over the last decade, Trump has played a prominent role in the spread of an intentional lie about American Muslims, one designed to malign Muslims as a category and Barack Obama as an individual. You've heard of this, of course: It's the conspiracy theory that Barack Obama wasn't really born in the United States, and that he doesn't have a genuine birth certificate, or his birth certificate has been doctored to create the false impression that Obama is an American citizen.

On Twitter, Donald Trump declared that "An 'extremely credible source' has called my office and told me that @BarackObama's birth certificate is a fraud." Elsewhere, Trump insisted that President Barack Obama, "doesn't have a birth certificate. He may have one, but there's something on that, maybe religion, maybe it says he is a Muslim. I don't know. Maybe he doesn't want that." Over and over again, for years, Trump told this story to anyone who would listen to it.

There are several manifestations of this conspiracy theory, and Donald Trump seems receptive to all of them. In one version, Barack Obama was born in Kenya, and was raised there as a boy to be a radical follower of Islam. In another version, Barack Obama was born in Cuba, and raised there as a boy to be a radical follower of Communism. In some versions, Barack Obama is alleged to be both a radical Communist and a fundamentalist

Muslim, even though those ideologies are inherently incompatible.

In most versions of the story, Barack Obama is alleged to be a secret agent, trained to go deep undercover in the United States, to run for President, and then let the enemies of America in to destroy everything from within. None of the people who have promoted these conspiracy theories have explained why, after seven years with Obama in the White House, and less than one year left to go, America hasn't been destroyed yet.

Barack Obama isn't Muslim. He showed the public his birth certificate years ago. These facts haven't deflated the blood libel of Obama as the bloodthirsty Muslim, though. That's because those who believe in the conspiracy theory are compelled by an emotionally-shaped idea that can withstand practically any rational refutation: the belief that only Christians of pure European ancestry are qualified to lead the nation. The promotion of that white supremacist belief, in itself, makes for a compelling convergence between the ideologies of the Nazis and the Republican Party.

The parallels don't end there, however. Trump, along with Ben Carson, a neurosurgeon who decided to run for the Republican presidential nomination, has repeated a new anti-Muslim blood libel, a tall tale about thousands of Muslims cheering in New Jersey as the Twin Towers of the World Trade Center were destroyed by terrorists on September 11, 2001. Trump has insisted that, "I watched when the World Trade Center came tumbling down. And I watched in Jersey City, New Jersey, where thousands and thousands of people were cheering as that building was coming down. Thousands of people were cheering."

There is no evidence at all of anyone cheering the fall of the Twin Towers across the river in New Jersey, much less a crowd of thousands of American Muslims holding an impromptu party in the streets. Furthermore, Donald Trump wasn't in Jersey City at the time that he claims he saw huge crowds there cheering the terrorist attack against the United States.

Later, trying to defend his story, Trump said that he had seen the Jersey City Muslim celebrations of the September 11 attacks on a television news report. Journalists have scoured all their stockpiles of footage from that day, however, and no one has been able to find any evidence that any such television broadcast ever took place.

Of course, it's not a complete lie to say that there are Muslims who want to commit acts of terrorist violence in the United States. There are a few. Their numbers, however, are extremely small. The actual risk of death by a Muslim terrorist attack in the United States is almost zero. The average annual number of people killed in the USA by Muslim terrorists is just two. Yes, that's right, two per year.

More people in the United States are killed by cows per year than are killed by Islamic militants.

What's more, the United States has suffered from terrorist attacks that have nothing to do with Islam at all. Timothy McVeigh and the Unibomber weren't Muslims, but they killed viciously nonetheless.

The blood libel made by Donald Trump and other opportunistic Republican politicians is that American Muslims are always just a hair's width from conducting a terrorist attack, and celebrate violence against Americans whenever it happens. "Trump and Carson here are playing a particularly nasty game," writes Benjamin Wittes, Senior Fellow in Governance Studies at that Brookings Institution. "They are fabulists of the worst kind - that is to say they are fabulists in the malicious denigration of others. They are making things up to stoke hatred and intolerance; they are little different in that regard from those who peddled lies about black men raping white women in the old South or those those who made up and stuck by blood libels in old Europe. These type of lies have consequences."

It wasn't just Jews that Adolf Hitler and the Nazis crafted libels against, of course. Another one of their targets were Democratic Socialists – a relatively liberal political party in the Weimar Republic. The Nazis accused them of seeking to destroy religion, and so cast themselves as the great defenders of Christianity.

"My feelings as a Christian point me to my Lord and Savior as a fighter," Hitler said. "We tolerate no one in our ranks who attacks the ideas of Christianity... in fact our movement is Christian." His opponents, warned Hitler, were radical atheists who had no respect for the role of religion in public life. "We were convinced that the people needs and requires this faith. We have therefore undertaken the fight against the atheistic movement," he said.

Donald Trump adopts a pose as the great defender of the Christian faith that is similar to Hitler's. "I'm proud to be a Christian, and as president I will not allow Christianity to be consistently attacked and weakened," he has declared. The fact that Christianity remains the most powerful religion in the United States doesn't seem to impact Trump's determination that it is in grave peril of being destroyed.

Among the supposed threats to Christianity that demands special attention from the President of the United States is the lack of adequately promotion of Christmas on the disposable coffee cups handed out at some coffee chains. Trump was outraged to hear that Starbucks coffee cups didn't offer a specific holiday greeting last year. "Did you read about Starbucks?" he angrily demanded of a crowd of supporters last December. "No more 'Merry Christmas' at Starbucks. No more. Maybe we should boycott Starbucks."

It seems silly, but Donald Trump's verbal assault against Starbucks coffee cups is part of a larger right wing narrative that re-emerges every year. It's a story of a War on Christmas.

The idea is that Christians are under siege in America. Socialist secular liberals are supposed to be on a campaign to wipe out the Christian religion, using department stores and coffee shops to do it. Every year, conservative Christian groups come out with lists of large businesses who are complicit in this supposed ideological assault. Their offense: In their advertisements and store displays in November and December, they don't use the word "Christmas" enough.

Christianity is in decline in the United States. Year after year, fewer people identify themselves as Christians, and more define themselves as unaffiliated to any religion. In reality, this change is part of a spontaneous shift away from a monolithic American cultural identity, toward an American identity more associated with experimentation, innovation and diversity. Donald Trump and his supporters don't see it that way, however. They perceive the change as the consequence of a centralized conspiracy by secretive elites, manipulating society away from acts of Christian worship by purposefully eliminating commercial messages with the phrase, "Merry Christmas".

Donald Trump's ideology is similar to that of the Nazis in that he perceives his culture, that of conservative, European-American Christianity, to be under siege. It isn't just secular liberals who are at the gates of Trump's cultural citadel, however. When he looks out from his fortress, Trump sees an army of dirty Mexicans coming to take away his wealth.

Trump began his presidential campaign with a volley of insults against Hispanics in the United States. In his announcement speech, he declared, "When Mexico sends its people, they're not sending the best. They're sending people that have lots of problems and they're bringing those problems. They're bringing drugs, they're bringing crime. They're rapists and some, I assume, are good people, but I speak to border guards and they're telling us what we're getting."

Trump wasn't the first person to complain about the cultural impurities brought into the United States by immigrants from Mexico. What most people don't realize is that Adolf Hitler was an early critic of the idea of an open border between the Mexico and the United States.

In Mein Kampf, Adolf Hitler wrote that, "Whenever Aryans have mingled their blood with that of an inferior race the result has been the downfall of the people who were the standard-bearers of a higher culture. In North America, where the population is prevalently Teutonic, and where those elements intermingled with the inferior race only to a very small degree, we have a quality of mankind and a civilization which are different from those of Central and South America. In these latter countries the immigrants--who mainly belonged to the Latin races— mated with the aborigines, sometimes to a very large extent indeed. In this case we have a clear and decisive example of the effect produced by the mixture of races. But in North America the Teutonic element, which has kept its racial stock pure and did not mix it with any other racial stock, has come to dominate the American Continent and will remain master of it as long as that element does not fall a victim to the habit of adulterating its blood."

Reading these words from Adolf Hitler, the ideological link between Trump and the Nazi Party comes into focus. Hitler hoped that the Nazi Party purge of non-German immigrants would be modeled upon America's creation of strong borders. Hitler continued, "I realize fully that nobody likes to hear these things. But it would be difficult to find anything more illogical or more insane than our contemporary laws in regard to State citizenship. At present there exists one State which manifests at least some modest attempts that show a better appreciation of how things ought to be done in this matter. It is not, however, in our model German Republic but in the U.S.A. that efforts are made to conform at least partly to the

43

counsels of commonsense. By refusing immigrants to enter there if they are in a bad state of health, and by excluding certain races from the right to become naturalized as citizens, they have begun to introduce principles similar to those on which we wish to ground the People's State."

Hitler, it seems, would strongly approve of Donald Trump's plan to expel 11 million Hispanics, and to build a gigantic border wall to separate the United States from the rest of the world.

Trump's vision of a purified America wouldn't exclude only Hispanics. He also has proposed a ban on all Muslims, prohibiting them from entering the United States. Trump would even outlaw Muslim American citizens from coming back into the United States after driving into Canada to see Niagara Falls. Trump sees no half measures in his campaign for the cultural purification of America, but calls his plan "a total and complete shutdown" of Muslim freedom of movement into the United States.

In his demand for a complete border shutdown, Trump depicts Muslims as foreigners. In fact, Muslims have been in the United States for as long as there has been a United States. Historical records show that Muslims were among those who fought for independence from England in 1776.

There is a strong vein of racism in Trump's denial of the deep historical role of Muslims throughout American history. Today, most Muslims in the United States are African-American. Anti-Muslim measures are thus a way to lash out at African-American communities.

It's particularly ironic that Donald Trump is now leading an authoritarian Christian campaign to ban Muslims from entering the United States when, for generations, it was authoritarian Christians who demanded the right to bring Muslims into the United States without restriction.

Of course, back then, the Muslims were brought into

the United States as property. They were brought into the United States, by force, as slaves.

The United States is like the Weimar Republic in that it carries the burden of a long, cruel history of racism and oppression of cultural minorities. The honored marble monuments of Washington D.C. were built by enslaved human beings. The unique America's popular music was born out of the isolation and despair of racial segregation and oppression in Jim Crow America.

Americans like to think of these problems as mere history, something that their nation has moved beyond. In February 2016, however, the Trump for President campaign provided an astonishing reminder that the USA is not a post-racism society after all.

It began when David Duke, a prominent white supremacist and former Grand Wizard of the Ku Klux Klan expressed his enthusiastic support for the Trump campaign. Duke, who had previously declared that "Our clear goal must be the advancement of the white race and separation of the white and black races. This goal must include the freeing of the American media and government from subservient Jewish interests," now urged his neoNazi supporters to sign up to volunteer at the nearest Trump for President campaign office. "Go in there, you're gonna meet people who are going to have the same kind of mindset that you have," Duke told them.

When Trump was confronted by a reporter about this endorsement by the KKK leader, he refused to distance himself from Duke. Trump, who had never hesitated to slam Muslims, Mexicans, women, or gays, expressed a sudden reluctance to rush to judgment of the leader of a violent white nationalist organization, saying, "Just so you understand, I don't know anything about David Duke, OK? I don't know anything about what you're even talking about with white supremacy or white supremacists. So I don't know. I mean, I don't know - did he endorse me or what's going on? Because I know nothing about David

Duke. I know nothing about white supremacists. And so you're asking me a question that I'm supposed to be talking about people that I know nothing about."

Trump pretended that he didn't know much about David Duke. However, in public comments 16 years before, Trump had acknowledged his familiarity with David Duke, and had properly identified Duke as a leader of racist organizations. It isn't easy to simply forget a neoNazi extremist like David Duke.

Over the very same weekend that he received the support of the KKK, Trump decided to forward a quote from Fascist dictator Benito Mussolini to his followers. The quote referred to the need for strong political leaders who are willing to feast upon the more vulnerable members of society: "It is better to live one day as a lion than 100 years as a sheep."

That the quote came from Mussolini, the Italian ally of Adolf Hitler during World War II, was quite clear. Trump had taken the statement from a Twitter account with the username @ilDuce2016. Benito Mussolini was known as Il Duce.

Trump's presidential campaign is thoroughly infused with racist ideology because Trump's strategy has been to use the legacy of popular racism in the United States to bring together a firm political base upon which to grow his candidacy. Adolf Hitler used a similar strategy in his own struggle to become the supreme leader of Germany.

Like the United States, Germany had a long legacy of pervasive racist ideology. Anti-Semitism was not the invention of the Nazis. Its practice went back at least as far back in time as the Crusades, when Germanic armies supposedly preparing to fight against Muslims in the Middle East went on bloody rampages against Jewish communities all along the way, starting in the area now known as Germany.

Martin Luther, the German leader of the Protestant Reformation, wrote a text called On The Jews And Their

Lies, in which he advised his Christian followers to "be on your guard against the Jews, knowing that wherever they have their synagogues, nothing is found but a den of devils in which sheer self-glory, conceit, lies, blasphemy, and defaming of God and men are practiced most maliciously and veheming his eyes on them."

Luther called upon his countrymen to begin a project of ethnic cleansing against the Jews. "Eject them forever from this country," he wrote. "For, as we have heard, God's anger with them is so intense that gentle mercy will only tend to make them worse and worse, while sharp mercy will reform them but little. Therefore, in any case, away with them!"

Luther was not content to merely encourage other Germans to persecute Jews. He personally led pogroms against them in several towns. Luther instructed the leaders of German cities to, "First to set fire to their synagogues or schools and to bury and cover with dirt whatever will not burn, so that no man will ever again see a stone or cinder of them. This is to be done in honor of our Lord and of Christendom, so that God might see that we are Christians, and do not condone or knowingly tolerate such public lying, cursing, and blaspheming of his Son and of his Christians... Second, I advise that their houses also be razed and destroyed. For they pursue in them the same aims as in their synagogues. Instead they might be lodged under a roof or in a barn, like the gypsies. This will bring home to them that they are not masters in our country, as they boast, but that they are living in exile and in captivity, as they incessantly wail and lament about us before God. Third, I advise that all their prayer books and Talmudic writings, in which such idolatry, lies, cursing and blasphemy are taught, be taken from them. Fourth, I advise that their rabbis be forbidden to teach henceforth on pain of loss of life and limb."

You get the idea. Luther goes on and on, describing the best way to persecute the Jews in extreme detail. One form of oppression Luther recommended that stands out in particular was the prohibition on Jewish travel between states. Luther's anti-Semitic travel ban and Donald Trump's proposed prohibition on Muslim travel are cut from the same cloth.

Just as Adolf Hitler's anti-Semitism arose out of a long history of discrimination, so has the racism of Donald Trump. The ugly American tradition of racial segregation for example, was echoed in Trump's early business career.

In 1973, the United States Department of Justice took the Trump Management Company, of which Trump was President, to court. The Trump Management Company was accused of apartment leasing discrimination against African-Americans. Investigators had uncovered a pervasive practice of lying to African-American families, telling them that none of Trump's apartments were available for lease, when in fact, there were many ready to be rented. Trump's business was also accused of charging higher fees and insisting upon stricter leasing terms to African-American families than it provided to European-American families.

The case was settled out of court. As part of the settlement, Trump agreed that his company would not discriminate against African-Americans, and would share records of the apartments his company had available. The Trump Management Company just couldn't keep from discriminating against African-Americans, however, and in 1976, Trump's business was brought back into court for continuing to practice illegal racist segregation in housing.

Donald Trump was practicing Jim Crow in New York City. The city's human rights commission had to send investigators to report on Trump's racist leasing practices for years.

It wasn't the last time his racism was exposed in public. In 1989, Trump expressed envy at the remarkable advantages that he believed come from being African-American, saying, "If I was starting off today, I would love to be a well-educated black because I really do believe they have the actual advantage today."

Is Donald Trump right? Do young African-Americans really have an advantage over young European-Americans?

It's now 27 years after Trump made his remark, and it's often said that racism in America isn't as bad today as it used to be. Nonetheless,

- African-Americans have just 2.7 percent of the wealth in our country, even though they are 13 percent of the population
- African-American children are punished 300% more often than European-American children
- African-American juvenile offenders are put on trial as adults more often than European-American juvenile offenders
- When African-Americans and European-Americans are sentenced for committing the very same crimes, African-Americans receive more severe punishments
- 37 percent of the people arrested for drug offenses are African-Americans, but African-Americans commit just 14 percent of drug offenses in the United States
- On average, African-Americans begin life in families with less money than European-Americans
- African-Americans are more likely to be searched when they are stopped for traffic violations than European-Americans are, and are stopped by police at a higher rate, even though they violate traffic laws at the same rate as European-Americans
- African-Americans are kept off of juries at a higher rate than European-Americans
- African-Americans with the same credit scores as European-Americans are more likely to have

their mortgage applications rejected
- People with names that are judged to sound African-American are less likely to be asked for job interviews than people with names that seem European-American, even when their resumes are exactly the same
- African-Americans are more likely to go to poorly-funded schools than European-Americans

These aren't the kinds of advantages that anyone would want to deal with. The kind of advantages that Trump had, like a father with a vast financial fortune, powerful friends at the top of New York City government, a swanky private school education, and a well-paying job guaranteed straight out of college, are more along the lines of what most people would like to have.

Trump's long public record of conspicuous racism and recent plans for new, government-sponsored systems of discrimination on the basis of ethnicity, religion, sexual orientation and disability have excited the members of extremist nationalist groups. Before the 2016 Trump campaign appeared, the membership of these groups had been sagging. Now, they're ramping up for a new round of white supremacist militancy, seeing Trump as their hero.

The American Nationalist Super PAC has paid to have explicitly racist pro-Trump robocalls to likely Republican voters in Iowa, New Hampshire, and Vermont with messages such as "We don't need Muslims. We need smart, well-educated white people."

In Minnesota, the PAC sent out this message to voters over the telephone: "The American Nationalist Super PAC makes this call to support Donald Trump. I am William Johnson, a farmer and white nationalist. The white race is dying out in America and Europe because we are afraid to be called racist. This is our mind-set: It's OK that our government destroys our children's future, but don't call me racist. I'm afraid to be called racist. It's OK to give away our country for immigration, but don't call me racist. It's OK that few schools anymore have beautiful white children in the majority, but don't call me racist. Gradual genocide against the white race is OK, but don't call me racist. I'm afraid to be called racist. Donald Trump is not a racist, but Donald Trump is not afraid. Don't vote for a Cuban; vote for Donald Trump."

Trump's openly bigoted way of talking breaks with a tacit understanding within the Republican party that dates back half a century, to a time when many Democrats disaffected by their party's support for feminism and civil rights shifted their party loyalty to the GOP. Republicans embraced the agenda of these racist and sexist Democratic defectors, but there was an unspoken rule. It was no longer acceptable to speak openly of African Americans as inferior. People could still express racist or sexist ideas, but they had to do so in code, with ideas like demographic problems, urban crisis, the cycle of poverty, how feminism had gone too far, or the negative effects of affirmative action.

Trump simply ignores these implicit codes. He doesn't talk about problems with "immigration," he calls immigrants criminals and rapists. Hillary Clinton wasn't defeated, she was "schlonged." He has brought back a kind of straight talk about race and gender that a lot of people have been missing.

It's become nearly impossible to keep up with the barrage of bigotry coming from the Trump for President campaign, it comes out so rapidly. In this sense, Trump seems to be applying Adolf Hitler's observation about the power of overwhelming verbal assault: In Mein Kampf, Hitler wrote that, "At a given sign it unleashes a veritable barrage of lies and slanders against whatever adversary seems most dangerous, until the nerves of the attacked persons break down... This is a tactic based on accurate estimation of all human weaknesses, and its result will lead to success with almost mathematical certainty."

Hitler's faith in the power of overwhelming aggression was not restricted to mere verbal rhetoric, of course. He urged the use of extreme physical violence in order to force enemies into submission. "Terror cannot be overcome by the weapons of the mind but only by counter-terror," he wrote.

Donald Trump expressed the same idea when he told his supporters that, "The other thing with the terrorists is you have to take out their families, when you get these terrorists, you have to take out their families." It's a war crime to purposefully target civilians in order to intimidate one's enemy. Donald Trump doesn't care for such restrictions, but it's important to remember what provoked the creation of the current international system of laws of warfare in the first place.

The Geneva Conventions of 1949 were created in reaction to the atrocities of World War II, many of which were committed by the Nazis. Convention IV explicitly forbids the execution of civilians, even in time of war. In rejecting this standard, and advocating for the assassination of the families of alleged terrorists, Trump is seeking to take the world back to the horrors of the 1940s.

Among the horrors created by the Nazis were concentration camps, where millions of people were starved, tortured, worked to death, or simply murdered. For Adolf Hitler, these camps were part of "the final solution".

Although he has yet to imagine a scope of concentration camps that would come anywhere close to the scale of those built by the Nazis, Donald Trump is an advocate for brutal prison camps of his own sort. In February 2016, Barack Obama declared that he would make a final effort to close the prison camps at the U.S. military base at Guantanamo Bay on the island of Cuba.

The Guantanamo Bay prison camps became infamous under George W. Bush, when it was revealed that prisoners there were subjected to repeated torture. Although the Bush Administration insisted that all of the people imprisoned in Guantanamo Bay were "the worst of the worst", for years there was no legal proceeding to determine whether there were any credible allegations against the prisoners at all. When military commissions finally were established as the sole legal proceedings available to prisoners in Guantanamo Bay, they shocked the world, seeming more like the kangaroo courts established by authoritarian regimes than anything else. The accused were deprived of full and independent representation before the tribunals. Evidence obtained under torture would be permitted, and the accused would in many cases not even be allowed to know what evidence was being used against them.

Many of the Guantanamo Bay prisoners had been captured far away from any battlefield, and so could not credibly be assigned the legal status of prisoners of war. What's more, the Guantanamo Bay prisons did not meet the standards of the Geneva Conventions, which include legal standards for the imprisonment of soldiers during war time. Many of the prisoners turned out to have no connection to terrorism at all, while others were only tangentially connected to organizations that themselves had connections to terrorism, and weren't personally involved in the planning or execution of terrorism. Some of the prisoners were children.

Donald Trump responded to the news of the White House's determination to close the Guantanamo Bay prisons by telling his supporters, "This morning I watched President Obama talk about Gitmo, right, Guantanamo Bay - which, by the way we are keeping open, and we're going to load it up with some bad dudes, believe me. We're going to load it up."

Trump's ideas for what to do with large number of "bad dudes" he plans to load into prison camps such as Guantanamo were made plain when he told another audience a story about a mass murder of prisoners of war attributed to General John Pershing.

"Early in this century, last century, General Pershing, did you ever hear? Rough guy. Rough guy. They had a terrorism problem, and there's a whole thing with swine and animals and pigs, and you know the story. They don't like them, and they were having a tremendous problem with terrorism, and by the way, this is something you can read in the history books, not a lot of history books, because they don't like teaching this, and General Pershing was a rough guy, and he sits on his horse, straight like a ramrod, and it was early 1900s, and this was a terrible problem.

They were having terrorism problems, just like we do, and he caught fifty terrorists who did tremendous damage and killed many people, and he took the fifty terrorists, and he took fifty men, and he dipped fifty bullets in pig's blood. You heard that, right? He took fifty bullets, and he dipped them in pig's blood, and he had his men load his rifles and he lined up the fifty people, and they shot forty-nine of those people, and the fiftieth person, he said: 'You go back to your people and you tell them what happened.'... So we better start getting tough, and we better start getting vigilant, and we better start using our heads, or we're not going to have a country, folks! We're not going to have a country."

This story combines a certain glee in the idea of forcing Muslims to violate the dictates of their religion with a disregard for basic human rights. Muslim religious leaders were outraged at Trump's delivery of this story, but explained that the horror Muslims feel in its telling comes from its glory in killing, not in the detail of dipping bullets in pigs' blood.

It may be easy for Trump to imagine such a scenario when all that he has seen of war have been Hollywood-produced fight scenes projected up onto a movie screen, but the plain fact is that the story Trump told about General Pershing is only a story. There is no evidence at all that any such event ever took place. It appears to be an urban legend, not actual history.

It's bad enough that Trump can't distinguish between fact and fiction. It's worse that the fictions Trump chooses to believe are sadistic.

It's a war crime to conduct mass executions of prisoners of war. Convention III of the Geneva Conventions specifically require the execution of prisoners of war without fair trial. The convention outlaws "the passing of sentences and the carrying out of executions without previous judgment pronounced by a regularly constituted court affording all the judicial guarantees which are recognized as indispensable by civilized peoples."

Three quarters of a century ago, the United States fought against Adolf Hitler so that atrocities such as mass executions would no longer take place. Donald Trump wants to bring these crimes against humanity back.

Trump's habit of celebrating cruelty and injustice, on the battlefield and in domestic life, that leads Danielle Allen, a political theorist at Harvard University, to conclude that, "Donald Trump has no respect for the basic rights that are the foundation of constitutional democracy, nor for the requirements of decency necessary to sustain democratic citizenship. Nor can any democracy survive without an expectation that the people require reasonable arguments that bring the truth to light, and Trump has nothing but contempt for our intelligence."

Trump's strategy seems to copy Hitler's skill at overwhelming his audience's capacity for reason with raw emotion, using the posture of fury as a political tool. Trump openly celebrates the power of anger.

Of 77 recent statements by Trump checked by PolitiFact, 76% were found to be mostly false or false-more than any other politician. Trump claims to have seen thousands of people in Jersey City cheering as the World Trade Center fell. He said the Mexican government sends "the bad ones" to the United States. He has lied about extremely trivial things, like denying he played golf with Samuel L. Jackson. He posted lies about black-on-white homicide statistics that came directly from a neo-Nazi with a swastika for an avatar who remarked that "we should have listened to the Austrian chap with the little moustache."

No evidence has ever been found to back up any of these claims made by Trump, and we live in an age when, with the Internet, checking simple facts is easier than has ever been before. So, every time Donald Trump has been caught in a lie, political commentators have predicted that his campaign would crumble as a result.

That still hasn't happened. To the surprise of many, repeated exposure of Trump's lies has had no impact on his popularity or credibility. He is still widely seen as straight-talking and genuine. A number of factors appear to contribute to this, all of which reveal the United States in the year 2016 to be fertile ground for the precipitous rise of a bigoted demagogue.

Trump has turned getting the facts wrong into an advantage. It supports his image as unscripted and unrehearsed. "Am I gonna check every statistic?" he asked Bill O'Reilly.

The typical presidential candidate is expected to verify facts before proposing policies aimed at changing them, but Trump has defined himself as an exception to the typical candidate. He doesn't lie in the way people are used to being lied to by politicians. He doesn't wait for results from focus groups and opinion polls, consult with handlers, then decide what to say. He simply talks. If he gets facts wrong, this only affirms his authenticity.

Trump seems to have learned from the example of authoritarian leaders like Benito Mussolini and Adolf

Hitler that getting the facts wrong matters much less getting the emotion right. Just as Mussolini and Hitler saw that anger was the emotion most helpful in summoning and maintaining popular support, Trump has decided that 2016 is the year when Americans must embrace their anger.

Trump embodies the rage that he wants to see in the world.

In the foreword to his most recent book, Trump warned that, "Some readers may be wondering why the picture we used on the cover of this book is so angry and so mean looking. I had some beautiful pictures taken in which I had a big smile on my face. I looked happy, I looked content, I looked like a very nice person, which in theory I am. My family loved those pictures and wanted me to use one of them. The photographer did a great job. But I decided it wasn't appropriate. In this book we're talking about Crippled America— that's a tough title. Unfortunately, there's very little that's nice about it."

The meme of a Crippled America justifies all sorts of abuse in Trump's nationalist ideology. Particularly troubling is the way that Trump encourages bigotry among America's children. The Nazis organized Hitler Youth organizations to indoctrinate young Germans in nationalist ideology. Today, Youth for Trump has formed on the social media site, spreading messages with hashtags such as #IslamIsTheProblem and #MuslimsGoHome.

Trump also shares the Nazi Party's affection for censorship as a tool for social control. He has urged the creation of new limits on freedom of speech, using protection from terrorism as an excuse. "We're losing a lot of people because of the Internet," Trump says. "We have to see Bill Gates and a lot of different people who really understand what's happening and maybe, in some ways, closing that Internet up in some ways."

Are we losing a lot of people because of the Internet? How many people are dead because of terrorists sending email through the Internet?

The reflex is to presume that terrorism is a serious problem, and that the threat of terrorism justifies the sacrifice of some constitutional rights. In politics, however, reflexes can be deceiving.

Think this through: Have you ever witnessed a terrorist attack? Do you know anyone who has been killed in a terrorist attack? Has there ever been a terrorist attack in your neighborhood?

For almost all Americans, the answers to these questions will be "no". The terrorist attacks of September 11, 2001 were dramatic and terrifying, but it turns out that they were not part of a larger trend. Terrorist attacks in the United States are actually extremely rare.

More Americans are killed by dogs than are killed by terrorists. No one is suggesting that we round up all the dogs and euthanize them, or put them into canine concentration camps.

So, why are so many Americans so eager to give up their constitutional rights in order to provide the feeling of protection from terrorism?

Adolf Hitler was an expert at conjuring enemies who were plotting the destruction of Germany. He convinced an entire nation to turn itself inside out in order to defend itself from Jews, who were actually just a small, peaceful, law-abiding minority.

How far will Donald Trump persuade Americans to go in order to protect themselves from a threat of terrorism so small that, in the last 20 years, only about 6 millionths of one percent of the U.S. population has fallen prey to it?

One destination Trump clearly plans to take America to in his pursuit of absolute security is financial bankruptcy. Trump is vague about many of his policies, but he has specific plans to imitate Hitler in one practical respect: He wants to dramatically increase military spending.

"I'm going to make our military so big, so powerful, so strong, that nobody, absolutely nobody is ever going to mess with us," says Trump. He says that the United States isn't "winning" enough because its military is too small.

Hitler made the same argument. He insisted that Germany would be saved only if it could rebuild a military stronger than any of its neighbors. In Mein Kampf, he complained, "Today our Left-wing politicians in particular are constantly insisting that their craven-hearted and obsequious foreign policy necessarily results from the disarmament of Germany, whereas the truth is that this is the policy of traitors. To all that kind of talk the answer ought to be: No, the contrary is the truth. Your action in delivering up the arms was dictated by your anti-national and criminal policy of abandoning the interests of the nation."

Of course, big military spending didn't lead Germany to security, to peace, or to prosperity. It led Germany into ruin and defeat.

The United States already has the largest and most powerful military in the world. America's military spending is larger than the military spending of all the other countries on Earth combined. Why do we need to make it even bigger?

Donald Trump doesn't just advocate for bigger spending on the military. He also proposes using it more. Trump is no isolationist. Instead, he shares Adolf Hitler's eagerness to send armies off to fight.

It's true that Trump has boasted about his supposed opposition to the 2003 military invasion of Iraq, citing it as evidence of his superior wisdom. However, it's important to note that Trump actually expresses that opposition in terms of the Iraq War in particular, not as an example of opposition to war in general.

Furthermore, in contradiction to the claims he has made while debating Jeb Bush, Trump didn't actually speak out in opposition to the invasion of Iraq. Back in 2002, when Congress was debating whether to approve George W. Bush's plan for a rushed bombing and invasion of the country, Donald Trump got on a nationally broadcast radio show and declared that yes, he thought that the plan to go to war in Iraq was a good idea. It seems that Trump's claims of having opposed the Iraq War, made during the 2016 campaign, were little more than a tactic to exploit Jeb Bush's greatest weakness.

The foreign policy that Trump advocates now is centered around intimidation and outright violence. Trump derides President Obama's renewed military attacks in Iraq, and expansion of American attacks into Syria, as not nearly aggressive enough. "Gentle bombing," Trump calls it, in comparison with what he would like to do.

"I've been saying bomb the oil for years," Trump says. "We're going to get rid of ISIS. We're going to get rid of them fast!"

Trump supporters are taking the cue. At a rally in Pensacola, Florida, a group of young girls wearing outfits with a gaudy American flag motif took to the stage before Trump himself appeared, to warm up the crowd. They sang praises for Trump's promises of more war in the near future.

The lyrics of their song: "Cowardice? Are you serious? Apologies for freedom, I can't handle this. When freedom rings, answer the call! On your feet! Stand up tall! Freedom's on our shoulders, USA. Enemies of freedom, face the music! Come on, boys, take them down! President Donald Trump knows how to make America great. Deal from strength or get crushed every time!"

Trump is gaining support for his plans for more war from more than just troupes of dancing girls, of course. Right wing religious leaders are echoing his drumbeat for more fighting as well. Baptist preacher Robert Jeffress, for example, gave a sermon to his followers declaring that, "Government is never called upon to forgive. Government is never called upon to turn the other cheek. The responsibility of government, according to the word of God, is to protect its citizens. And one way the government protects its citizens is by securing the borders... You may not agree with everything Donald Trump says, but Donald Trump was absolutely right when he said, 'It is time to start bombing the you-know-what out of ISIS.' That is a biblical response."

Many Christians will be shocked to see a preacher from their own religion promoting the blatant sadism of Donald Trump. It's worth remembering, though, that the Nazi Party in Germany received a great deal of support from Christian individuals and organizations there, even when some dissident churches were targeted for destruction.

Turning the other cheek is a quiet act that usually doesn't earn much attention. A louder voice from American Christianity demands the righteous punishment of the wicked. Such is the Christianity of Donald Trump.

In Trump's ideology, righteous punishment includes the infliction of pain for its own sake. Trump, like Hitler, believes in the power of torture.

The last Republican president, George W. Bush, personally ordered the torture of prisoners. That torture was illegal, and ineffective. It never resulted in the revelation of information that could prevent a terrorist attack.

However, at least when torture was conducted under George W. Bush, it had a purpose. The Bush Administration acknowledged in the abstract that torture was illegal, and played rhetorical games to claim that the special techniques American soldiers and intelligence agents applied against prisoners, designed to cause pain, terror and psychological suffering, were not torture.

Donald Trump has removed all of those veils, and nakedly promises that, if he is elected President, yes, the U.S. government will torture people.

"Would I approve waterboarding? You bet your ass I would. In a heartbeat! I would approve more than that," Trump told the audience at a recent political rally. Even if it doesn't work, they deserve it anyway!"

Like Hitler did, Trump depicts vulnerability as a moral fault, and argues that the "winners" in society have the right to power. He writes, "America needs to start winning again. Nobody likes a loser and nobody likes to be bullied. Yet, here we stand today, the greatest superpower on Earth, and everyone is eating our lunch. That's not winning."

Trump wouldn't merely approve the use of torture. He wouldn't do it reluctantly. He would do it eagerly. Trump would agree to the torture of people in a heartbeat. Even if it "doesn't work", if there is no possible practical benefit to torture, Donald Trump would have it done.

How is that any different from the cruel fascination with pain cultivated by the Nazi Party?

Like Hitler, Trump isn't concerned with compassion. He wants to win, and will use whatever tactics he believes will enable him to win.

"I will do whatever it takes," says Trump. Whatever it takes could include many terrible things.

Winning is everything for Trump. As a consequence, he respects leaders who display strength more than he respects leaders who work for openness, tolerance, and freedom. In the abstract, respect for strong leaders might sound like a positive trait. In application, however, centralization of power in the hands of an unrivaled executive can lead to disaster. Yet, this is just what Donald Trump is aiming to achieve in taking the presidency for himself. David Harsanyi, editor at The Federalist, calls this totalitarian ideology "Trumpism – a philosophy based on the vagaries of one man".

In 1990, Trump was interviewed by Playboy magazine. That year, the old Soviet Union was finally opening up to the rest of the world. Some of the old republics were beginning a retreat back into dictatorship, but Russia was out of the grips of Stalinist Communism.

Trump approved of the ending of the Soviet Union, but he didn't approve of the weakening of the country's centralized leadership. Rather than seeing the spread of protests as a sign of strengthening political liberty, he perceived them as a sign that Mikhail Gorbachev wasn't an adequate leader. "Their system is a disaster. What you will see there soon is a revolution; the signs are all there with the demonstrations and picketing. Russia is out of control and the leadership knows it. That's my problem with Gorbachev. Not a firm enough hand," Trump told Playboy.

The consequences for the people of the Soviet Union would be dire, Trump warned. Political protest would inevitably lead to a violent revolution overthrowing Gorbachev, Trump warned, saying, "I predict he will be overthrown, because he has shown extraordinary weakness. Suddenly, for the first time ever, there are coal-miner strikes and brush fires everywhere- which will all ultimately lead to a violent revolution."

There was an attempted coup d'etat in the Soviet Union the year after Trump made this prediction. It wasn't a violent revolution led by angry workers, however. It wasn't an extension of street protests. It was a bloodless coup made by hardline Soviet leaders, strongmen of the sort that Trump said Gorbachev needed to become. They wanted to re-impose all of the authoritarian Soviet structures that Gorbachev had been working to dismantle. They failed.

It was, in part, political protests in the streets of Moscow that ended the 1991 coup against Gorbachev. The strongmen ended up as, to use Trump's vocabulary, "the losers".

Mikhail Gorbachev did lose power, but he relinquished it peacefully, not at gunpoint. Gorbachev didn't give up power to an authoritarian determined to restore centralized power across the Soviet Union. He gave way to Boris Yeltsin, who became the first political leader of the new Russia.

Trump's prediction that freedom to protest would lead

to violent revolution in the Soviet Union was wrong. Everyone makes incorrect predictions some of the time, of course. What's relevant for Americans' efforts to understand Trump in 2016 is the nature of the prediction that he chose to make back in 1990. When he interpreted Gorbachev's moves toward democracy as signs of weak leadership, Donald Trump revealed a belief that authoritarianism is the most effective style of government, and that strongmen make the best leaders.

This faith in antidemocratic authority was revealed by another comment made in the Playboy interview. Trump declared admiration for the Chinese government's bloody crackdown against student protesters in Tiananmen Square. Trump suggested that it had been a mistake to allow the protests to grow as large as they had, saying, "When the students poured into Tiananmen Square, the Chinese government almost blew it. Then they were vicious, they were horrible, but they put it down with strength. That shows you the power of strength."

Then, Trump made a comment that has become a drumbeat in his 2016 presidential campaign: "Our country is right now perceived as weak… as being spit on by the rest of the world."

CONCLUSION

Only by understanding how those who seek the power try to influence us, and how we often actively participate in our own manipulation, can we finally understand the dangers we face if we leave rationality and skepticism behind and, instead, put our faith in a leader with charisma." – Laurence Rees

It's obvious that Donald Trump is not Adolf Hitler. Trump would not replicate the exact policies and practices of Adolf Hitler if he were to be elected President of the United States. Trump was born the year after Hitler killed himself. He's an American. Hitler was German. Trump was born with millions. Hitler was born dirt poor.

These distinctions aren't the point. People who compare Trump and Hitler aren't proposing that Trump will soon walk out before television cameras with a swastika arm band tied over his jacket. As Mark Twain noted, history does not repeat itself, but it does rhyme. As we compare Trump and Hitler, we are looking for rhymes.

The historical, biographical and social distinctions between Donald Trump and Adolf Hitler are stark. However, they are not complete. When people compare Trump to Hitler, they're trying to understand whether Donald Trump might be the sort of person who, when granted power, could engage in the level of brutality that Hitler unleashed upon the world.

So, when people ask Steve Ross, who studies the history of fascism at the University of Southern California, whether Donald Trump is a fascist, Ross's response is to say no, because fascism was something very specific in the political history of the 20th century. Donald Trump isn't a fascist. He isn't a Nazi. He's something else, a new kind of brutal authoritarian leader, with similarities to fascists, but with new, cruel tendencies of his own.

Ross notes, upon reflecting on the actions and words of Trump on the campaign trail, "We had the same thing happening in Germany in the 1920s with people being roughed up by the Brownshirts and they deserved it because they were Jews and Marxists and radicals and dissidents and gypsies. That was what Hitler was saying... I'm not saying Trump is Hitler, but the logic of condoning violence against those who oppose you -- you can imagine, a man who would condone it as a candidate -- what would he do as an official president?"

What would Donald Trump do as President?

It would be profoundly unwise for Americans to evaluate the people who present themselves as candidates for President only according to what they say they would do. Wise voters know that presidential candidates often make many promises on the campaign trail that they do not follow through with once they move into the White House.

We try to judge the character of presidential candidates by comparing them to previous political leaders. We seek out similarities between current candidates and political leaders in the past whose achievements we admire. We skeptically examine politicians for signs of dangerous tendencies by looking for echoes of the despots of the past.

Donald Trump is not Adolf Hitler. Donald Trump is, in some important ways, like Adolf Hitler.

It's not just liberals who are concerned about Donald Trump's nationalist extremism. Weeks before the Republican primaries began, Max Boot, a senior member of the Council on Foreign Relations, wrote, "Trump is a fascist. And that's not a term I use loosely or often. But he's earned it."

David Boaz of the libertarian Cato Institute cautions that, "Not since George Wallace has there been a presidential candidate who made racial and religious scapegoating so central to his campaign. Trump launched his campaign talking about Mexican rapists and has gone on to rant about mass deportation, bans on Muslim immigration, shutting down mosques, and building a wall around America. America is an exceptional nation in large part because we've aspired to rise above such prejudices and guarantee life, liberty, and the pursuit of happiness to everyone. Equally troubling is his idea of the presidency - his promise that he's the guy, the man on a white horse, who can ride into Washington, fire the stupid people, hire the best people, and fix everything. He doesn't talk about policy or working with Congress. He's effectively vowing to be an American Mussolini, concentrating power in the Trump White House and governing by fiat."

Gospel musician Kirk Franklin writes, "To every pastor that stood next to Donald Trump last week, I hope you now see why we're losing respect as Christians in the world... While you were so busy wanting 'camera time,' you didn't 'take time' to examine his character... Banning Muslims does not reflect our country, or our Christ. I am very disappointed in people that say they believe what I believe compromise that for contaminated influence. I'm done."

Christine Todd Whitman, a Republican former governor of New Jersey, comments, "Frankly, if you go and look at your history and you read your history in the lead-up to the Second World War this is the kind of rhetoric that allowed Hitler to move forward, because you had people who were scared the economy was bad, they want someone to blame."

Thomas Sowell of the conservative Hoover Institution warns that, "No doubt much of the stampede of Republican voters toward Mr. Trump is based on their disgust with the Republican establishment. It is easy to understand why there would be pent-up resentments among Republican voters. But are elections held for the purpose of venting emotions? No national leader ever aroused more fervent emotions than Adolf Hitler did in the 1930s. Watch some old newsreels of German crowds delirious with joy at the sight of him."

Any single similarity between Adolf Hitler and Donald Trump is, in itself, insignificant. The identification by any particular political group of a Trump-Hitler parallel could be easily dismissed. What we're seeing in the comparisons between Trump and Hitler in the context of the 2016 presidential race is on an entirely different level.

Never have so many different comparisons between an American presidential candidate and Adolf Hitler been made. It isn't just Trump's policies that are being linked to Hitler's. His language, his manners, his mannerisms, his political tactics, his supporters' behavior, his biographical and social connections are being noted as well. American liberals, conservatives, moderates, historians, artists, Holocaust survivors, and foreign leaders are taking note of the similarities.

The comparisons come along with increasingly fervent demands that no political leader ever be compared to Adolf Hitler. Those who make these demands for silence recognize that when the memory of Hitler is brought into a political conversation, a profoundly unsettling shift takes place.

We cannot blame people for being disturbed when Donald Trump is compared to Adolf Hitler. We can take a critical perspective, however, and try to evaluate the source of their unease.

As unsettling as it is to consider the possibility that a democratically-elected politician could exploit our support, and use the power of our government in order to commit atrocities, it is the responsibility of voters in a democracy to make such considerations.

Despite Trump's claims that we are a ruined nation that must be made great again, the United States of America is the most powerful nation that has ever existed, with a military more deadly than any other in human history. Any person who seeks executive authority over the USA must be subjected to the harshest scrutiny.

Instead of blaming those who take note of similarities between Donald Trump and Adolf Hitler for our discomfort, American voters should face their feelings of unease. We should expand our skepticism rather than suppressing it, so that every presidential candidate, not just Donald Trump, is subjected to the Hitler Test.

Let's talk more about the atrocities committed by Adolf Hitler and the Nazis, and the other authoritarians of the past. Instead of turning away, and pretending that the Holocaust was some unique aberration, and that Hitler was an unexplainable manifestation of pure evil, let's rededicate ourselves to understanding how the Nazis rose to power and used it to such terrible ends. Let's look at the many other instances of popularly-supported atrocities too, so that we understand the symptoms of growing totalitarianism.

Most importantly let's reject the temptation to imitate Adolf Hitler ourselves. Let's avoid the easy path of attributing all evil to a single scapegoat, and casting it out of our sight to gain an irrational feeling of protection from it.

We must not pretend that Donald Trump alone represents the only voice of violent nationalism in the United States. His growing power is merely a manifestation of a more pervasive hardening of American culture. Just as Hitler did not rise to power on his own, neither can Donald Trump ascend to the Oval Office without the votes of millions of Americans.

As we note the similarities between Donald Trump and Adolf Hitler, we must also cast a critical gaze at ourselves. How much, each one of us should ask, am I similar to a citizen of the Third Reich? In the candidate I support, in the speeches I applaud, how far along the path toward authoritarian nationalism have I gone?

Doubt, but don't despair. As you compare yourself to a person in the crowd at a rally in Nazi Germany, listening to Adolf Hitler speak, recognize the opportunity for resistance as well, and ask yourself: What am I willing to do to take a stand against this?

AFTERWORD:
ON TRUMP AND REALITY

David Byrne has suggested another reason that Trump supporters are "so seemingly unaware of his lies and bullshit, and the ridiculousness of many of his positions and ideas." Social media tends to present a "point of view that you already agree with, since you only see what your 'friends' are sharing. We all do this to some extent - your friends share news with you and presumably many of your friends share your viewpoints. The algorithms built into those social networks are designed to reinforce this natural human tendency and expand upon it - if you like this, you'll like this. The networks reinforce your existing point of view in order to give you more of what you like, as that will make you happy and keep you on the network - and, in turn, more ads can be accurately targeted your way."

People who disagree with Trump tend to have networks of friends who disagree with Trump, and tend to follow sources that disagree with Trump. The information they receive through social media will have a strong tendency to be critical of Trump. Their initial exposure to a statement made by Trump is likely to be critical, or indicate that it has already been debunked. This tendency extends to news sources that are linked to by their friends and referenced in the sources they follow. For people who agree with Trump, it is precisely the opposite. The information they receive through social media will have a strong tendency to present Trump in a positive light. If a claim made by Trump has been debunked, they are much less likely to hear about it.

Daniel Patrick Moynihan famously remarked that "You are entitled to your opinion, but you are not entitled to your own facts." This is changing as social media develops the ability to target fact claims to people who are already predisposed to accept them. Beliefs are reinforced whether or not they are true, while evidence challenging those

71

beliefs becomes increasingly less visible. Different views arise not just from different frames of interpretation, but from different sets of fact claims. It becomes harder and harder for people to understand how someone could possibly hold different beliefs.

This dynamic may be part of the reason that so many people enthusiastically support Trump, while so many remain completely bewildered at how anyone could possibly find him credible. It may also be a reason he is in danger of remaining underestimated until it is too late.

Assuming that Trump and his supporters are simply engaged in building beliefs based on fact claims may distract us from important aspects of his appeal. Drawing on Roland Barthes, Judd Legum has commented on a way that Trump, a member of the World Wrestling Entertainment (WWE) Hall of Fame, has been conducting his campaign. While the other candidates have been acting like boxers, Trump has been acting more like a professional wrestler.

"This public knows very well the distinction between wrestling and boxing; it knows that boxing is a Jansenist sport, based on a demonstration of excellence. One can bet on the outcome of a boxing-match: with wrestling, it would make no sense. A boxing-match is a story which is constructed before the eyes of the spectator; in wrestling, on the contrary, it is each moment which is intelligible, not the passage of time… The logical conclusion of the contest does not interest the wrestling-fan, while on the contrary a boxing-match always implies a science of the future. In other words, wrestling is a sum of spectacles, of which no single one is a function: each moment imposes the total knowledge of a passion which rises erect and alone, without ever extending to the crowning moment of a result."

Pundits accustomed to the traditional rules of a presidential campaign have been observing for months that Trump has lost. In July of 2015, the New York Post called him "toast" after he insulted John McCain for his capture in Vietnam.

Trump's insult was outrageous. It broke the rules-not just the rules presidential campaigns are supposed to play by, but basic principles of humanity and decency.

In a typical campaign, such a blatant violation of the rules would signal a loss, but Trump isn't mounting a typical campaign. In Trump's campaign, as in professional wrestling, being outrageous and breaking the rules is how you win. Professional wrestling is a kind of theater in which larger-than-life champions of good square off against exaggerated caricatures of evil. According to this code, the hero wins by transgressing the rules of a corrupt system.

"Some fights," Barthes observes, "among the most successful kind, are crowned by a final charivari, a sort of unrestrained fantasia where the rules, the laws of the genre, the referee's censuring and the limits of the ring are abolished, swept away by a triumphant disorder which overflows into the hall and carries off pell-mell wrestlers, seconds, referee and spectators."

As with the rigged rules of the game a wrestling hero rebels against, American politics is perceived by Trump's supporters as a corrupt system. Voting is presented as a way for citizens to exercise power, but this is increasingly viewed as an illusion concealing a corrupt reality that denies power to the average citizen. Party insiders, wealthy donors, super PACs, and other shadowy power brokers make the real decisions behind the scenes.

Trump's supporters see the electoral system as a kind of theater with a predetermined outcome. Their engagement with democracy, in this way, is not so different from watching a professional wrestling exhibition.

DAMAGE HAS ALREADY BEEN DONE

The future of a Trump presidency is a dreadful prospect, but what we face in Donald Trump is not just something to fear in the future. The harm caused by his campaign is a reality that has been unfolding over months.

Consider the example of Mercutio Southall, a protester who was attacked at a Trump Rally in Birmingham, Alabama.

Southall suffered a concussion, but the damage inflicted in the attack goes beyond that. His attack came not just at the hands of security, but also from members of the crowd. He was not just forcibly removed from the event. He was thrown to the ground, kicked, punched, choked, and called racist epithets including "monkey" and "nigger."

Trump's comment when asked about Southall was this: "Maybe he should have been roughed up." The attack against Southall is not the only time racial violence has been perpetrated by Trump supporters. Trump's comments afterwards were not the only time he has sanctioned racist violence.

Racist mob violence does more than hurt bodies. It sends a message of degradation and intimidation to all members of the minorities that come under attack. It emboldens people to make similar attacks in the future, while causing entire populations to live in fear.

Hitler's violence against racial minorities is remembered for its institutional efficiency. But before there was Auschwitz, there was Kristallnacht. The night of November 9, 1938 is known as "crystal night." The name comes from shards of glass from the smashed windows of Jewish homes, businesses, and synagogues. The destruction was perpetrated by citizens and brownshits, while government officials looked on and allowed it to proceed.

Dozens were killed on Kristallnacht, but the damage

went beyond that. The message was sent to ethnic and religious minorities that they could be harmed with impunity.

If elected, Trump promises to create a "deportation force" to round up and expel eleven million undocumented immigrants from the United States within a period of two years. This forced expulsion would be comparable in scale to the one carried out by Hitler. It would require the creation of an extensive system of detention facilities and a huge police force whose sweeping raids would devastate families and communities inside the United States. Outside the United States, it would create a massive humanitarian crisis as millions of deportees flood into Mexico. This has not yet come to pass, but its very proposal has already led to widespread insecurity and fear.

Tremendous harm has already been caused by Trump's sanction of racist mob violence, insults against religious and ethnic minorities, and threats of the detention and deportation of millions.

It is not too late, however, to turn aside the growth of Trumpist nationalism. We still have time to prevent further harm, if we accept that the threat has become serious, and is no longer in the category of crude antics displayed by a reality TV show clown.

OTHERS' STATEMENTS ON TRUMP

Statement from the American Civil Liberties Union:

"Donald Trump's proposal to bar Muslims from entering our country based solely on their faith is blatantly unlawful and fundamentally un-American. We are a nation of immigrants, many of whom came to this country to escape prejudice and discrimination. We urge all of our political leaders to categorically reject this dangerous escalation of hateful rhetoric because it undermines our core American values."

Letter to Donald Trump from the Muslim Public Affairs Council:

"Ever since you announced your run for Presidency of the United States, you have scapegoated the American Muslim community and other minority groups for all your perceived ills of America.

The truth is that you – and your supporters -- are scared of anything that is different than you.

You rely on the promotion of fear and Internet lies to fuel the flames of hate and divisiveness across our country.

You have no understanding of the world in which you live. That's why you insist on backward policies, such as building walls and segregating communities based on religion, as a desperate attempt to create a false sense of strength and security, and to preserve your distorted view of what makes America great.

Well, we have news for you: We will no longer be bullied. We will no longer be your punching bag.

We challenge you to a debate with a representative from the American Muslim community on the issues you have raised about Islam and Muslims.

We are confident that you, a person of great rhetorical

ability, will appreciate this opportunity to showcase to America your strength and knowledge in such matters."

Statement by Council on American-Islamic Relations Chair Nihad Awad:

"Donald Trump's inflammatory rhetoric has crossed the line from spreading hatred to inciting violence. By directly stating that the only way to stop terrorism is to murder Muslims in graphic and religiously-offensive ways, he places the millions of innocent, law-abiding citizens in the American Muslim community at risk from rogue vigilantes. He further implies that our nation should adopt a strategy of systematized violence in its engagement with the global Muslim community, a chilling message from a potential leader. We pray that no one who hears this message follows his gospel of hate."

From A Letter to Donald Trump from Amara Majeed:

With all due respect, Mr. Trump, you are a demagogue who is capitalizing on Americans' fear and paranoia; you are scapegoating an entire population of 1.6 billion people in an attempt to further your campaign, in an attempt to "make America great again." But the effect of this is that by advocating for the registration of Muslim Americans and the banning of Muslims from entering the United States, you are providing a platform on which the marginalization of and discrimination against an entire group of people becomes justifiable, even "American." I could go on about how problematic it is that you equate the actions of a small extremist group with nearly a fourth of the world's population, but I find it to be of even greater interest that white supremacists are actually greater perpetrators of domestic terrorism compared to Muslim terrorists…

You are dragging the American people back into the past, keeping us from moving forward. I have always believed that the rent I pay for being privileged enough to grow up in the United States is to contribute to the advancement of modern American society. And that's the thing, Mr. Trump: You can never take that away from me.

From the Anti-Defamation League:

"Donald Trump's hate speech against immigrants is highly inappropriate and we join with the voices of many others around the country who have condemned his offensive remarks. It is time for Trump to stop spreading misinformation and hatred against immigrants, legal and undocumented."

From Political Theorist Danielle Allen:

"Like any number of us raised in the late 20th century, I have spent my life perplexed about exactly how Hitler could have come to power in Germany. Watching Donald Trump's rise, I now understand."

From the United Kingdom's Prime Minister David Cameron:

"I think if he came to visit our country he'd unite us all against him."

From the Human Rights Campaign:

"Donald Trump has pandered his way to the top of the field by opposing the most basic protections for LGBT people and supporting Kim Davis-style discrimination against LGBT people," said Human Rights Campaign President Chad Griffin. "What's more, despite being married three times himself, this is a candidate who says he looks forward to appointing justices who would overturn marriage equality for loving same-sex couples. Donald Trump's calculated efforts to use division, fear and bigotry to score political points is as dangerous as it is vile."

Shakira Testifying about Trump:

"This is a hateful and racist speech that attempts to divide a country that for years has promoted diversity and democracy. No one living in this century should stand behind so much ignorance."

J.K. Rowling on Trump:

"Voldemort was nowhere near as bad."

Praise for Donald Trump from retired Ku Klux Klan Grand Wizard David Duke:

"The Jewish knives are coming out on Donald Trump. How come it's against America values to want to preserve the heritage of the country? We're overwhelmingly a Christian country and overwhelmingly a European country."

BIBLIOGRAPHY

Armstrong, K. (2001). Holy war: The Crusades and their impact on today's world. New York: Anchor Books.

Ayçoberry, P. (1999). The social history of the Third Reich: 1933-1945. New York: New Press.

Blair, G. (2000). The Trumps: Three generations that built an empire. New York: Simon & Schuster.

Flood, C. B. (1989). Hitler, the path to power. Boston: Houghton Mifflin.

Gonen, J. Y. (2000). The roots of Nazi psychology: Hitler's utopian barbarism. Lexington, KY: University Press of Kentucky.

Hitler, A., & Murphy, J. V. (2011). Mein Kampf: The official 1939 edition. Arden, Warwickshire: Coda Books.

Johnson, E. A., & Reuband, K. (2005). What we knew: Terror, mass murder and everyday life in Nazi Germany: An oral history. Cambridge, MA: Basic Books.

Kaufman, M. T. (2003). Soros: The life and times of a Messianic billionaire. New York: Vintage Books.

Noakes, J., & Pridham, G. (1975). Documents on Nazism, 1919-1945. New York: Viking Press.

Rees, L. (2012). Hitler's charisma: Leading millions into the abyss. New York: Pantheon Books.

Shirer, W. L. (1960). The rise and fall of the Third Reich; a history of Nazi Germany. New York: Simon and Schuster.

Trump, D., & McIver, M. (2004). Trump: How to get rich. New York: Ballantine Books.

Trump, D. (2011). Time to get tough: Making America great again! Washington, D.C.: Regnery Publishing.

Trump, D. (2015). Crippled America: How to Make America Great Again. New York: Threshold Editions.

Trump, D. (2015). Donald Trump: Make America Great Again. Capitol Publishing.

Photo by Gage Skidmore

Photo by Heinrich Hoffmann, in the public domain

ABOUT THE AUTHOR

Horace Bloom is an electrical engineer, history buff, and amateur alpaca farmer living outside Eugene, Oregon. He is registered to vote as neither a Democrat nor a Republican, has much less than a billion dollars in assets, and has no ambition either to become a painter or to be elected to public office.